MIGRATION AND EMPIRE 1830–1939

Simon Wood

The front cover shows the Cunard liner Queen Elizabeth, the largest liner ever built, being launched from the John Brown & Co. shipyard in Clydebank in 1938. The shipyard opened in 1871 and was best known for its liners and warships. The insert image shows a poster for the Anchor-Donaldson line, which began operating passenger services between Glasgow and Canada in 1916, using ships built on the Clyde in Glasgow.

The Publishers would like to thank the following for permission to reproduce copyright material:

Photo credits p.2 © Paisley Museum & Art Galleries, Renfrewshire Council; p.3 © Royal Commission on the Ancient and Historical Monuments of Scotland; p.6 © Royal Commission on the Ancient and Historical Monuments of Scotland; p.8 © The Print Collector / Heritage Images; p.12 © Royal Commission on the Ancient and Historical Monuments of Scotland; IN/903; p.15 © Scottish Life Archive, National Museums of Scotland; p.21 Courtesy of Archives of Ontario; p.22 © National Records of Scotland, AF51/91/1; p.24 © National Records of Scotland, BR/GSW/4/18; p.26 © National Records of Scotland, AF51/158; p.28 © Culture and Sport Glasgow (Museums); p.34 Courtesy of GoogleBooks / Scottish Reformation Society; p.35 © Church of Scotland; p.37 © Grand Orange Lodge of Scotland; p.41 © Glasgow City Archives; p.44 © North Lanarkshire Council; p.45 © Scottish Life Archive, National Museums of Scotland; p.47 © Dundee City Council, Central Library, Photographic Collection; p.54 © Hudson Bay Company Archives, Archives of Manitoba; p.56 Courtesy of Wikipedia Commons; p.57 Courtesy of Wikipedia Commons; p.59 © McCord Museum; p.63 © MelbourneLibrary; p.64 © Allan C Green Collection, State Library of Victoria; p.65 Courtesty of Wikipedia Commons; p.67 © Mary Evans Picture Library; p.68 © Australian War Memorial; p.70 © Hulton-Deutsch Collection/CORBIS; p.71 © Voyager New Zealand Maritime Museum; p.72 © Mary Evans Picture Library; p.74 (top) © INTERFOTO / Sammlung Rauch / Mary Evans, (bottom) © Dunedin City Council; p.77 © Getty Images; p.79 © Duncan Walker –iStockphoto; p.80 © Duncan Walker –iStockphoto; p.84 The Print Collector / Alamy; p.85 © Hibernian Football Club; p.86 © Gallacher Memorial Library - Glasgow Caledonian University Library; p.87 Courtesty of Wikipedia Commons; p.88 © Scottish Life Archive, National Museums of Scotland; p.89 © Sharon McTeir; p.90 © Scottish Jewish Archive; p.91 © Scottish Life Archive, National Museums of Scotland; p.93 (top) © Glasgow Digital Library, based at the University of Strathclyde, (bottom) © Glasgow Digital Library, based at the University of Strathclyde; p.94 Courtesy of Steven Bradley (http://www.flickr.com/photos/39245032); p.97 © Duncan Walker –iStockphoto; p.98 © National Museums Scotland; p.101 © Glasgow Museums; p.102 © Bridgeman Art Library / Fleming-Wyfold Art Foundation; p.104 (top) © Alexander Turnbull Library, National Library of New Zealand, (bottom) © Alexander Turnbull Library, National Library of New Zealand; p.112 © Culture and Sport Glasgow (Museums).

Orders: please contact Bookpoint Ltd, 130 Milton Park, Abingdon, Oxon OX14 4SB. Telephone: (44) 01235 827720. Fax: (44) 01235 400454. Lines are open 9.00–5.00, Monday to Saturday, with a 24-hour message answering service. Visit our website at www.hoddereducation.co.uk. Hodder Gibson can be contacted direct on: Tel: 0141 848 1609; Fax: 0141 889 6315; email: hoddergibson@hodder.co.uk

First published in 2011 by
Hodder Gibson, an imprint of Hodder Education,
An Hachette UK Company
2a Christie Street
Paisley PA1 1NB

Impression number 5 4 3 2 1
Year 2014 2013 2012 2011

Cover photo © Topical Press Agency/Stringer/Getty Images; © Culture and Sport Glasgow (Museums)(insert)
Illustrations by Jeff Edwards and Pantek Media
Typeset in Sabon 11pt by Pantek Media, Maidstone, Kent
Printed in Italy

A catalogue record for this title is available from the British Library

ISBN: 978 1444 124378

Contents

Introduction

Who is this book for?

The books in this series are for students following the new Scottish Higher History Course. Each book in this series covers all you need to know about one of the most popular topics in Paper 2 of the newly revised Scottish Higher History course. The entire syllabus is covered so you can be sure all your needs will be met.

What is in this book?

From 2011, Paper 2 of your Higher History exam is completely different from any earlier Higher History exam paper. There are five completely new Scottish-based topics. These topics are:

- The Wars of Independence 1286–1328
- The Age of the Reformation 1542–1603
- The Treaty of Union 1689–1740
- Migration and Empire 1830–1939
- The Impact of the Great War on Scotland 1914–1928

Each topic is divided into six issues. Check out the SQA website at: http://www.sqa.org.uk. There you will find detailed descriptions of the content that is in each and every topic in Paper 2.

The first issue you will see is called 'Background'. The last issue is called 'Perspective'. Neither of those issues will have any questions asked about them. They are NOT examined. That leaves four other issues, and each one of those issues has a question linked to it.

Topic: Migration and Empire 1830–1939	
Background	looks at the social effects of the development of the Scottish economy: industrialisation and urbanisation; the imperial context.
Issue 1	considers push and pull factors in internal migration and emigration: economic, social, cultural and political aspects; opportunity and coercion.
Issue 2	looks at the experience of immigrants, with reference to Catholic Irish, Protestant Irish, Jews, Lithuanians and Italians; the reactions of Scots to immigrants; issues of identity and assimilation.
Issue 3	considers the impact of Scots emigrants on the growth and development of the Empire with reference to Canada, Australia, New Zealand and India in terms of: Economy and enterprise, Culture and religion, and Native societies.
Issue 4	looks at the contribution of immigrants to Scottish society, economy and culture; the impact of Empire on Scotland.
Perspective	considers the significance of migration and Empire in the development of Scottish identity.

What do I have to do to be successful?

In Paper 2, all assessments will be in the form of questions based on primary or secondary sources. In this series there is full coverage of all four types of questions you will meet. You will have five sources to use and four questions to answer.

You will have 1 hour and 25 minutes to do that. That means you will have about 20 minutes to deal with each question so answers must be well structured and well developed. Put simply, that means you must do three things in each question:

1 You must do what you are asked to do.
2 You must refer to information in the source.
3 You must also include your own relevant recalled knowledge, where appropriate.

In the final chapter of this book there are not only examples of questions, but also full explanations of what makes good and not so good answers to the differing questions. Each type of question has its own particular process you must use to answer it successfully. In this section you will also find clear explanations of how marks are allocated so that your answers can be structured to gain the best possible score.

What types of questions will I be asked?

There are FOUR different types of question. Each type will be in your exam paper.

Question Type 1 is a source evaluation question worth 5 marks. It will usually be identified with a question asking, 'How useful is Source A as evidence ...'

In this type of question you are being asked to judge how good the source is as a piece of historical evidence.

Question Type 2 is a comparison question worth 5 marks. You will be asked to compare two points of view overall and in detail. The question will not use the word 'compare' in the question.

The wording of the question could be something like 'To what extent do Sources B and C agree about ...'

Question Type 3 is a 'How far' question and is worth 10 marks. This question is to test your knowledge on one specific part of an issue, called a sub-issue. You can find all the sub-issues in the column called 'detailed descriptors' on the SQA syllabus website at: **http://www.sqa.org.uk**.

Question Type 4 is a 'How fully' question and is worth 10 marks. This question is to test your knowledge of a whole issue. Remember there are four issues in the syllabus on which you can be examined

To summarise ...

This book will help you to be successful in Paper 2 of the Scottish Higher History course. To be successful you must recognise the type of question you are being asked, follow the process for answering that type of question and also show off your own knowledge of the topic.

Beware: The four question types explained here **WILL** appear in the exam paper every year but will **NOT** appear in the same order every year. You will need to stay alert and be ready for them in any order.

1 Background: Scotland in 1830 and beyond

Source 1.1

Land use potential in Scotland

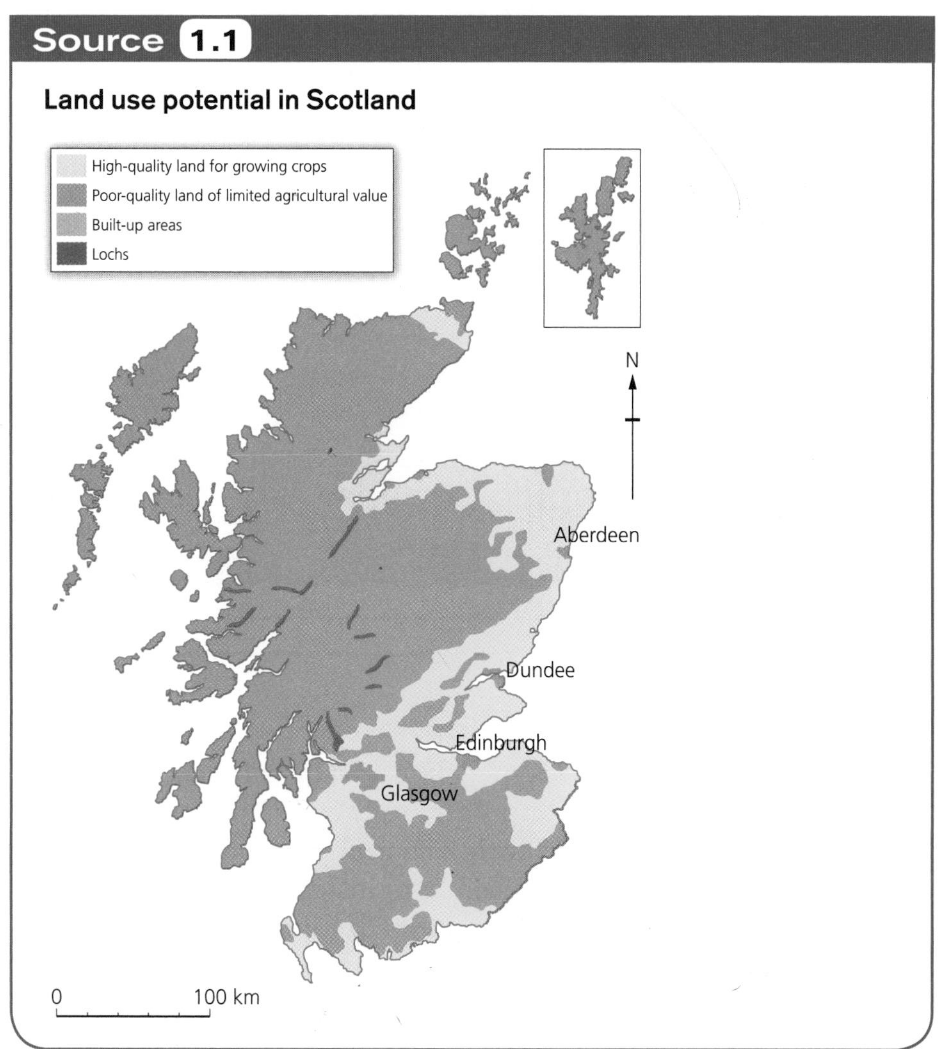

Scotland is a country that has been shaped by the movement of people into and out of it. There are many reasons to explain why this happened. Probably the most important reason was economic change. By 1830 the process of industrial change in Scotland was well underway. For most Scots industrial change meant changes to the way they worked and the places where they worked. During the nineteenth century many Scots found work in factories, mines and shipyards. The industrial revolution meant that factories became the places for mass production of goods. The first industry to undergo industrialisation was textile manufacture with the introduction of machines to weave and spin cloth.

Source 1.2

Factory chimneys, Paisley, Renfrewshire, 1887

Industrialisation

By 1830 the textile industry, and especially cotton manufacture, was Scotland's most important industry. By the end of the nineteenth century Scotland became globally important in a number of other industries. Heavy industries such as iron works and engineering increased in importance. By 1913, Glasgow and its surrounding towns produced one third of the railway locomotives built in Britain and 50 per cent of engines for British shipping. The number of ships built on the Clyde was one fifth of world production.

In the 1860s the American Civil War disrupted the import of cotton to Scotland so other types of cloth became important. As a result there was a growth in demand for other products like jute. Dundee became a world leading centre for the production of jute, and became known as 'Juteopolis' as a result.

Coats of Paisley dominated the thread-making industry and made 80 per cent of all thread produced in the world. Other parts of Scotland such as the Borders were important for the production of knitted goods, tweeds and tartans. At Clydebank the American Singer company employed over 10,000 people to produce sewing machines.

Source 1.3

Dundee saw its population triple between 1841 and 1901 as it became the leading producer of jute products. By 1900 over 50,000 people were employed in over 100 mills in the city, like the Tay Works, shown below.

One of the most important effects of industrialisation was the development of a better communication system that allowed goods produced in Scotland to be moved about the country quickly, as well as being sent overseas (see Source 1.4).

Source 1.4

Historian Michael Lynch describes communication developments:

'By 1845, the great "mania" of railway development had begun. The race to reach England was underway between two rival railways. The Caledonian Railway opened a west-coast route via Carlisle in 1848. Suddenly the journey time between London and Edinburgh or Glasgow [was] reduced from forty-three hours to seventeen; by the 1880s fierce competition had reduced it to eight hours.

Within Scotland, the railways [reduced] costs, encouraged economic growth and brought together the expanding urban network. Perishable goods could be transported long distances, migrants became more mobile.'

The development of a 'world' economy

Railway building meant that the Scottish economy was connected to England and the wider world as trade expanded. The development of large efficient steam ships, often built in Scottish shipyards, led to a huge expansion in trade with the Empire and beyond. British exports were worth £48 million in 1848. This had expanded to £136 million by 1860. Much of this wealth was created by Scots. Other Scots showed what the development of a 'world' economy could mean. For example, Thomas Lipton created a retail empire across Britain. He is perhaps most famous for the product Lipton's tea. This showed the close connection between Scotland and the Empire as the tea was supplied by plantations in Ceylon (modern-day Sri Lanka), which was then part of the British Empire.

Source 1.5

Historian Tom Devine sums up the importance of Scotland's economy:

'Coal, iron, steel, shipbuilding and engineering took off and transformed Scotland into a manufacturer for the world. All these sectors and others were committed to the export market. A small country of fewer than 5 million people in the 1900s emerged as a key player in the global economy, linking the primary producing regions of America, Africa, Australasia and Asia to the industrializing regions of Europe. Such a development was bound to have deeply significant effects on the nature and structure of Scottish society.'

This changing economy had four main effects according to historian Tom Devine.

Population growth

The first was a large increase in the population. Between 1831 and 1931 the population of Scotland more than doubled from just under 2.5 million to almost 5 million. Immigration had a part to play in this increase, in particular that of the Irish attracted by jobs in the Scottish economy.

Population movement

Secondly, the movement of people within Scotland increased as population moved to the central belt in search of job opportunities. Both Edinburgh and Glasgow, as well as their surrounding areas, saw significant population growth.

Farming

Thirdly, agriculture as an employer went into decline at the same time as mining, building and factory-based manufacturing grew. In the middle of the nineteenth century, 30 per cent of men working in Scotland worked

directly in farming, and most rural areas had been enjoying a rising population for a century. However, by the beginning of the twentieth century, only 50 years later, only 14 per cent of men working in Scotland found jobs in farming. By 1951 the figure had fallen to less than 10 per cent.

Urbanisation

Urbanisation means the growth of towns. As many Scots continued to move into towns looking for work, Scotland saw continued urbanisation. By the 1930s 63.4 per cent of Scotland's people lived in towns and cities of over 5000 inhabitants. This compares with just 31.2 per cent of the population in 1831. Most growth was in and around the four big cities of Glasgow, Edinburgh, Dundee and Aberdeen. At the beginning of the twentieth century one in three Scots lived in these cities. Glasgow, with its developing heavy industry, saw massive growth as the demand for skilled and unskilled labour increased. The population of Glasgow was over one million by 1931. However, growth was also swift in Aberdeen, which grew to 170,000 by 1931; Edinburgh had a population of 439,000 by 1931; and Dundee had a population of 176,000 by 1931.

Living conditions in the towns

The fast growth of towns led to overcrowding and dreadful living conditions in slums for many workers. Housing for the working class was particularly bad. The census of 1861 showed that 34 per cent of all Scottish houses had only one room; 37 per cent had two rooms. One in every hundred families lived in houses without any windows at all! The appalling conditions inside these houses can be seen in the quote from William Mitchell in 1886 (Source 1.6).

Source 1.6

William Mitchell describes conditions in Glasgow housing in 1886:

'In some rooms may be found many articles – old beds, tables, chairs, boxes, pots and dishes, with little regard to order or cleanliness. In other rooms we saw a box or barrel for a table, a broken stool, an old pot or pan, with a few dishes. In many rooms there was no furniture at all. The whole family, including men, women and children, huddled together at night on such straw or rags as they can gather.'

Living in such conditions meant that there was no privacy, no play area for children, nowhere to relax and nowhere to work. It was little wonder many men spent time in the pub where it was warm and well-lit, offering the chance of escape from conditions at home.

Death was all too common in such an environment, especially for children. Even then there was no privacy. Glasgow's first full-time Medical Officer for Health, Dr J.B. Russell, described how dead children were treated.

Source 1.7

Dr J.B. Russell states:

'Their little bodies are laid on a table or dresser so as to be somewhat out of the way of their brothers and sisters, who play and sleep and eat in their ghastly company.'

People lived in such conditions because it was cheap. Such a slum also had little heating or lighting costs. A tenement flat was surrounded on all sides by other properties. When it got dark the people lived in gloomy darkness or just slept.

Source 1.8

High Street Vennel, Glasgow, 1880s

Disease was widespread in the growing towns. There were cholera epidemics in 1832, 1848 and 1853 as well as typhus epidemics in 1837 and 1847.

Source 1.9

The reporter for the West of Scotland Handloom Weavers Commission said of Glasgow:

'I have seen human degradation in some of its worst phases but I can say that I did not believe until I visited the wynds of Glasgow that so large an amount of filth, crime, misery and disease existed in one spot in any civilised country.'

One of the reasons the Scots developed such a modern industrial system was because pay was low. People who moved from the Highlands and Ireland were willing to work for low wages. Cheap labour in textiles, mines, iron foundries and shipbuilding meant cheap products.

Industrial developments meant that Scottish resources, such as coal and ironstone, could be used efficiently. Between 1830 and 1844 iron output increased from 40,000 tons a year to 412,000 to give just one example. However, by the early twentieth century it was clear that Scotland relied on too few heavy industries for its economic well-being. With the decline in demand for ships and the rise of foreign competition the iron and coal industries were badly affected.

Scotland and the British Empire

In 1707 Scotland and England had become one nation with the union of the Parliaments. One of the benefits of this was that it gave Scotland unlimited access to England's colonial empire.

Throughout the nineteenth century Scots helped to develop the Empire, and the Scottish economy was boosted hugely by trade with the Empire. Ambitious Scots found jobs in India and North America in particular. Glasgow merchants became dominant in the tobacco trade and the profits they made helped turn Glasgow into the 'second city of the Empire' (after London). The Empire also offered opportunities for Scots to serve in the army. Highland and Lowland regiments were recruited and used widely in the expansion of the Empire. With their distinctive appearance Scottish soldiers added to their reputation as fierce fighters and were important in the expansion of the British Empire.

By 1830 most parts of the Empire were governed from Britain but the next hundred years saw a great deal of growth and change in the Empire – and Scots were very involved in these changes.

Source 1.10

A sergeant from the Argyll and Sutherland Highlanders in the mid-1800s. His uniform shows his proud Scottish identity.

Source 1.11

The British Empire around 1830

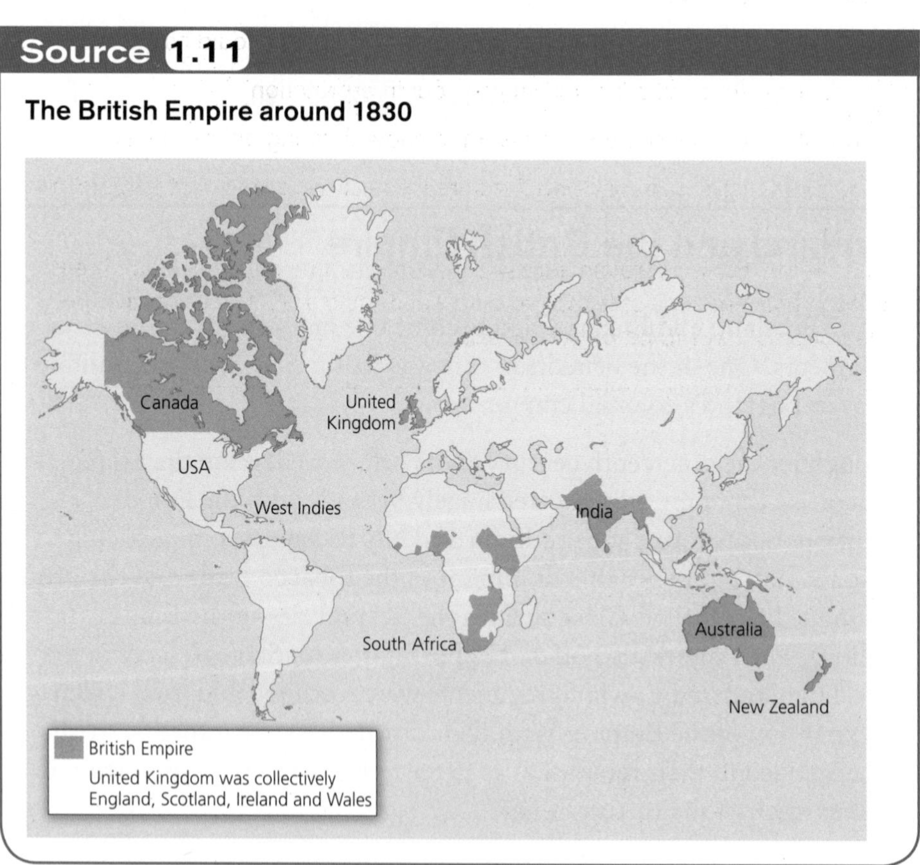

Activities 

Scotland in 1830

Your challenge is to produce a display or presentation showing the main features of Scotland in 1830 and developments that were having an effect on it. Your display or presentation must be eye-catching and make people want to stop and look.

Work in a group of no more than four. Your teacher will give you an appropriate time scale for the task.

Store your display in a safe place. You will do a similar exercise at the end of this course and you will be asked to compare the two displays and reach conclusions about the impact of migration and Empire on Scotland.

Your display or presentation should deal with the following topics.

- Scotland: the land
- Industrialisation and Scotland
- Urbanisation and Scotland
- The British Empire and Scotland

Success criteria

Somewhere in your display or presentation each topic should have:

- a four-sentence text box explaining your interpretation
- one illustration – or two if you want to show differing points of view
- a smart slogan summarising the core issue associated with the topic in your view.

Your display must be visible across a classroom. It must use at least three colours and must use at least two different sizes of text. Think creatively – this does not have to be paper based.

2 The migration of Scots

The historian Marjorie Harper has calculated that approximately two million people emigrated overseas from Scotland between 1830 and 1914. A further 600,000 Scots migrated to England in search of work. After a lull in movement caused by the First World War, Scots were on the move again with over half a million leaving before the outbreak of the Second World War in 1939. Many other European countries, such as Ireland and Norway, saw huge movements of population at this time. However, the Scottish experience was different from that in Ireland and Norway. This was because a very large number of Scottish emigrants were from urban centres. Emigration from Ireland and Norway was mostly rural. Also, a large proportion of Scottish emigrants were well educated or had skills that were wanted abroad. In this sense the Scottish experience is unique, as historian Tom Devine has noted.

Source 2.1

Historian Tom Devine states:

'Scotland was almost alone among European countries in having experienced both large scale industrialisation and a great outward movement of population. Most other societies prone to high levels of emigration were poor rural economies. It seems that many Scots were voting with their feet in the search for better prospects than were easily available to them at home.'

Economic reasons for migration

There were four periods when emigration was particularly large scale from Scotland. These were during the 1850s, 1870s, the early 1900s and between the two World Wars. In general these were times when the country was suffering economic problems. The rural Highlands were affected most in the 1850s, foreign competition hit farming in Scotland in the 1870s and the fishing industry was also affected in the 1880s and after the First World War. The decline of heavy industry in the central belt of Scotland after the First World War meant that industrialised urban Scotland suffered in the economic depression of the 1920s and 1930s. All areas of Scotland were

affected by emigration, but some events are remembered more than others. One event that still causes a huge amount of emotional debate is the Highland Clearances.

The Highland Clearances

The rural economy of the Highlands saw great changes from the eighteenth century onwards. Put simply, the land in the Highlands could not cope with the growth in population from the late eighteenth century. A population increase in the Highlands meant that the land was divided and subdivided between the increasing numbers of tenant farmers or crofters. With each generation, each crofting family got less and less land to survive on. The result was poverty. The crofters could not afford the rents charged and this led to reductions in rental income for the landowners.

The poverty of the Highlands can be seen in the poor quality of housing and in the limited diet of its population. The famous blackhouses of the West Highlands were homes of rough stone and turf, with heather thatch pegged to a few roof timbers, without a ceiling or paved floor, and without windows or a chimney. Animals shared the building with the humans in order to keep warm.

Source 2.2

Crofting Township, near Gairlochy, Highland, 1883

There is a lot of evidence of the poverty of the Highlands from the *New Statistical Account*, which was completed by parish ministers across Scotland. The *New (or Second) Statistical Account of Scotland* was published between 1834 and 1845. It aimed to provide a true account of the state of Scotland. The Church of Scotland ministers in their different parishes recorded the geography, population and industry of their areas. This account is considered to be the most accurate view of Scotland because the ministers wrote down the changes in their parishes compared with the *First Statistical Account* produced by Sir John Sinclair between 1791 and 1799.

One way in which Highland communities survived was by growing potatoes.

Source 2.3

The minister for Morven in Caithness noted in the *New Statistical Account*:

'there are many, it is feared, much in the predicament of a little boy of the parish, who, on being asked on a certain occasion of what his three daily meals consisted gave the same unvarying answer, "mashed potatoes", and on being further asked, "what else?" replied with great ... surprise, "a spoon".'

In 1846 potato blight wiped out the potato crop on the west coast of Scotland, leaving 150,000 people at risk of starvation.

Famine placed huge pressures on the financial resources of the landowners. Most of the relief funds that were offered to the starving Highland population came out of the landowners' pockets. Many landowners, such as MacLeod of MacLeod, went bankrupt as a result. Their lands passed into the hands of trustees, who along with the surviving landowners sought to make their land more profitable. Firstly, they encouraged the trade in cattle to feed the growing cities, then they brought in sheep, and eventually they changed the use of the land to deer hunting. In order to do this, land had to be cleared of the existing tenant farmers or crofters. By the 1830s the most famous of the Highland Clearances in Sutherland was over, but the problems of the Highland economy and for the landowners had not gone away. The historian Michael Lynch suggests that a collapse in the Highland economy forced landowners to rethink how best to use their land.

Collapse of the Highland economy

Source 2.4

Historian Michael Lynch states:

'Kelp prices fell steadily but slowly after 1810, but the bottom fell out of the market in 1827. There was, over the same period, a slump in cattle prices. Wool prices fell, as did those for sheep. By 1827 landowners were beginning to rethink the basics of the economy of their estates. A government report of 1841 concluded that the West Highlands now suffered from over population, on the huge scale of between 45,000 and 60,000 people. The Highland "problem" had materialised.'

Eventually all landowners turned to emigration as a way to remove the excess population and try to make their estates profitable. Often the landowner paid the costs of crofters travelling from Scotland to the colonies. For example, James Matheson, the landowner on the island of Lewis, paid for people to leave the land and even cancelled debts that were owed to him. By 1856 he had encouraged over 2200 crofters to leave Lewis.

It has been calculated that the Western Highlands lost one third of their population by 1861. Historian Eric Richards describes the main destinations of this displaced population, and why the Highland Clearances are still remembered by many today.

Source 2.5

Historian Eric Richards states:

'The people evicted in the classic period of the clearances [between 1790 and 1855] were often relocated within the estates of the landlord; many shifted off to neighbouring estates or counties; many families eventually made their way to Glasgow, Edinburgh and Dundee, joining the factory workforce ... [M]any of the women became domestics for the wealthy new bourgeoisie [middle classes] of urban central Scotland. Others migrated abroad, becoming Highlanders of eastern Canada, New Zealand, the United States and Australia. Many nurtured grievances which they passed on to their children and to their children too.'

Why are the Highland Clearances remembered with such a sense of grievance?

Many Highlanders who were forced to leave their homes felt betrayed by the landowners. Public opinion at the time of the clearances was firmly in support of those being evicted. The landlords and their agents, called factors, were blamed. The image of poor people being pushed off their land to make way for profit led to rage.

Source 2.6

Evicted family, Lochmaddy, Outer Hebrides, 1895

The geologist Sir Archibald Gieke saw one of the clearances at Suishnish on Skye. He described the moment of eviction (Source 2.7).

Source 2.7

Sir Archibald Gieke describes a clearance:

'A strange wailing sound reached my ears at intervals on the breeze from the west. On gaining the top of one of the hills, I could see a long and motley procession winding along the road. It was a miscellaneous gathering of at least three generations of crofters. There were old men and women, too feeble to walk, who were placed in carts; the younger members of the community on foot were carrying their bundles of clothes and household effects, while the children, with looks of alarm, walked alongside. When they set forth a cry of grief went up to heaven.'

He also knew who to blame!

Source 2.8

Sir Archibald Gieke:

'The land belonged to Lord Macdonald, whose affairs were in such a state that he had to place himself in the hands of trustees. These men had little knowledge of the estate. The interests of the crofters formed a very secondary consideration. The trustees determined to clear out the whole population of Suishnish and convert the ground into one large sheep farm.'

Crofters' Holdings Act of 1886

There can be no doubt that many clearances were carried out using force.

Although the worst of the clearances was over by the 1850s, they continued until the passing of the Crofters' Holdings Act of 1886. This Act gave crofters much greater rights over their crofts, by:

- establishing an independent body to fix rents
- giving security of tenure to crofters who paid the newly determined 'fair' rents
- allowing crofters to hand on their crofts to their children by inheritance.

Migration from the countryside to the towns

Although the first major migration and emigration of Scottish people was from the Highlands, all areas of Scotland were affected by population movement. Before the 1890s both the rural Highlands and rural parts of the Lowlands of Scotland saw similar drops in their population. The historian Christopher Smout has calculated this at about 9 per cent of the rural population. However, in the years between 1891 and 1931, when the Highland population was protected from eviction by the Crofters' Holdings Act, the population continued to drop at an increased rate. Smout calculates that the population of the Highlands and Islands fell by 26 per cent in this period, while that of the rural Lowlands fell by only 16 per cent. He uses this to support the argument that many left the Highlands and Islands willingly.

Economic factors were probably the most important reason for people leaving rural areas. For example, fishing was important to the Highland economy. The Brand Report of 1902 estimated that the average Lewis

family gained an income of about £3 annually from the sale of croft produce. On the other hand they gained £25 from fishing, which shows how important the fishing industry was to their income. When the Russian Revolution of 1917 brought an end to the large East European export trade in herring, the men who worked on trawlers and the women who worked as fish gutters lost their jobs.

Migration from rural areas to the growing towns and cities offered more opportunities for work. The towns also offered more opportunities socially. Life there was seen as exciting compared with the dull life in the countryside.

Source 2.9

An often quoted source from the 1893 Royal Commission on Labour states:

'A young woman will hand over her kist [box of clothes] to the porter, get her ticket for Glasgow, pull on her gloves, laugh and talk with her parents and comrades, jump into the train and thank her lucky stars that she is at last leaving the unwomanly job for domestic service and town society.'

The attractions of urban life over the rural were clear to many who lived on the land.

Source 2.10

The 1893 Royal Commission on Labour states:

'There is much drudgery and very little excitement about the farm servant's daily duties. Only slight importance is attached to the healthy character of country life in comparison with various branches of town labour. Only the shorter hours, numerous holidays and ever present busy bustle and excitement of town life, are present to the mind of our young farm servant.'

Sources 2.9 and 2.10 illustrate the fact that life in the country working the land was hard work, with long hours and few holidays. For example, before 1914 a ploughman would rise at 5 a.m. to feed and groom his horses. He worked until 6 in the evening, with a break between 11 and 1, an 11-hour working day. After the First World War this was reduced to 10 hours a day, and a Saturday half-day was given for the first time. Before this, the only holidays were Sundays, New Year's Day and the hiring days.

Pay was poor, and life in the countryside offered limited opportunities for socialising. As a result, when the chance arose, many rural workers wanted to leave for the bright lights of the town.

The mechanisation of agriculture also forced people to move. Steam power led to the introduction of threshing machines, and by the 1870s harvesting in the Lowlands of Scotland was a largely mechanical operation requiring far fewer hands on the farms. The mechanisation of farming had begun long before the mid-nineteenth century, but the impact on jobs only came in the 1860s.

Source 2.11

The historian Michael Lynch comments:

'Substantial shedding of labour came only after a series of technological innovations in the three decades after 1860, which saw the introduction of steam threshing, steam ploughing and machine reaping.'

The movement of population from the countryside to the town eventually led to a labour shortage in the countryside by the late nineteenth century. This shortage of manpower was dealt with largely through the introduction of labour-saving machinery. This further reduced opportunities for those who wanted to stay.

Further mechanisation continued into the twentieth century with the introduction of diesel power, the tractor and the combine harvester. All these developments made farmers far less reliant on muscle power.

The historian Tom Devine makes the further point that farming also supported a number of industries, such as the blacksmith, to maintain the metal ploughs and shoe the horses used in farming. These crafts were undermined by the effects of industrialisation.

Source 2.12

Tom Devine states:

'The development of branch railway lines enabled cheap factory goods to penetrate far into the rural areas and so threatened the traditional markets for tailors, shoemakers and other tradesmen. The displacement of craftsmen and their families from the smaller country towns and villages became a familiar feature of the rural exodus by the end of the nineteenth century...'

Devine argues that Lowland workers' attitudes were also very important. In the twentieth century, the young in particular did not find country employment particularly attractive. It was isolated and lacked access to leisure opportunities such as the pub, cinema, dance hall and football ground. Pay for country jobs did improve, and jobs such as being a shepherd were both well paid and had status, but they were simply not attractive to young people at a time when popular culture was growing and they heard of a brighter and better life by reading newspapers and listening to the radio.

Source 2.13

Tom Devine argues:

'Compared to the life of hard toil on the land, the town occupations of domestic servant, railway porter, policeman and carter seemed infinitely less demanding. Not only did they pay better than agricultural labouring in some instances, but they also had shorter hours, more leisure time and freedom in the evenings and weekends from employers.'

By the early twentieth century rural depopulation was still a feature of the changing pattern of Scotland's population.

Internal migration to England

The other part of Britain that Scots migrated to in large numbers was England. Scots offered a variety of skills that were attractive, and England offered higher wages and better opportunities in trades and professions.

Scottish farmers were well known for their expertise in farming, and many moved to England to set up farms. By 1930, 22 per cent of farmers in Essex, in the south of England, were immigrants and a very high proportion of these were Scots. Locals spoke of a 'Scotch' colonisation of Essex. One English commentator in 1902 described England as a 'Scot-ridden country', because there were so many! One other career where Scots were very visible was the medical profession. Scottish universities produced high-quality graduates in medicine, who were in demand. The historian Marjorie Harper illustrates how important Scots were in medicine.

Source 2.14

Marjorie Harper states:

'Medical schools and infirmaries in Liverpool, Manchester, Birmingham and Sheffield were all founded by Scots. Most of these doctors had been trained at Edinburgh or Glasgow, but the first eye hospital in London was founded by an Aberdeen graduate, John Farre.'

London was the most popular place for Scots to go to, as it is today. Many returned, but the vast majority stayed and integrated into English society.

Emigration

Although migration to the cities and England was very popular, many Scots chose to leave the British Isles altogether. Places like the United States, Canada, Australia and New Zealand were popular for Scots to emigrate to because of the widespread availability of land and the opportunity to earn more money. Different destinations were popular at different times. Canada was the destination of choice for Scots in the 1840s and in the period leading up to the First World War. Australia and New Zealand were popular in the 1850s and 1860s because of the discovery of gold! Even earlier than this, some Scots were forced to migrate to Australia whether they wanted to or not!

Leaving to go to prison!

Up to 1867 Australia was used as a place to send people convicted of crimes in Britain. Sending criminals to these prison colonies was called 'transportation'. The use of Australia for transportation started in 1787. Of 160,000 convicts transported from Britain to Australia only 5 per cent or about 7600 were Scottish. A transportation prison sentence could be for seven years, fourteen years or life. Many convicts chose to settle in Australia when they had served their time in prison, and there is evidence of families moving from Scotland to join them.

Leaving to gain freedom

Some Scots left because they wanted more freedom politically, socially or to worship their religion freely. These emigrants tended to be literate and come from jobs that had a tradition of self-help and political awareness. Skilled workers like the handloom weavers were an example of this. Industrialisation had affected them badly as they were replaced with the factory-based power loom. Canada was a popular destination, mainly because it was the easiest colonial territory to get to. It has been calculated that 22,000 Scots had arrived in Nova Scotia by 1838.

Letters home from emigrants show how Scots enjoyed the freedoms offered abroad.

Source 2.15

Neil Calder, from Bonar Bridge, emigrated to Australia. Writing home to his brother in 1899, he explains:

'The laws of Australia are very liberal and if anything at all lean to the side of the working class.'

Leaving for landownership and better prospects

Source 2.16

Canadian poster encouraging Scots to emigrate for landownership

Scots were popular emigrants. Many had skills that could be used in the developing economies of America and the Empire. Scots were good farmers and also possessed industrial skills that could be used abroad.

One example that shows how colonial development deliberately targeted the skills of Scots involved the British–American Land Company which was set up in 1833–4. The company bought one million acres of land in the Canadian province of Quebec from the Government. The company needed people to work the land in order to improve it and make it profitable.

It began to recruit the farmers that it needed. To begin with, the company helped 60 families from the Outer Hebrides with the cost of their passage across the Atlantic. In the following years more Highlanders followed and a sizeable Gaelic-speaking community developed in Canada.

Source 2.17

Information notice for Scottish emigrants

EMIGRANTS' INFORMATION OFFICE, 31, BROADWAY, WESTMINSTER, S.W.

1st October, 1905.

Office Open—
Every week day but Saturday 10.30 a.m. to 6.30 p.m.
Saturday 10.30 a.m. to 2 p.m. only.

GENERAL INFORMATION FOR INTENDING

EMIGRANTS

TO

CANADA, THE AUSTRALASIAN AND SOUTH AFRICAN COLONIES.

LENGTH AND COST OF PASSAGE.

The Time ordinarily taken on the voyage, and the lowest rate of unassisted passages to the above Colonies, are as follows:—

	BY STEAMER.		BY SAILING VESSEL.	
	Average Time.	Lowest Fare. (Liable to change) £ s. d.	Average Time.	Lowest Fare. (Liable to change) £ s. d.
CANADA	9-10 days	4 0 0	—	—
NEW SOUTH WALES	45-52 "	15 14 0	About 3 months	13 13 0
VICTORIA	42-49 "	14 14 0	Nearly 3 months	13 18 0
SOUTH AUSTRALIA	40-46 "	14 14 0	" 3 months	12 12 0
QUEENSLAND	56 "	15 15 0	About 3 months	15 5 0
WESTERN AUSTRALIA	33-40 "	16 16 0	" 3 months	14 14 0
TASMANIA	40-50 "	14 14 0	" 3 months	14 12 0
NEW ZEALAND	45 "	16 16 0	" 3 months	13 13 0
CAPE	20 "	13 15 0	—	—
NATAL	26-28 "	18 18 0	—	—

PASSAGES.

1. FREE PASSAGES. — QUEENSLAND. — To selected unmarried Agricultural Labourers and single Female Domestic Servants (apply to the Agent General). No Free Passages to any other Colony.

2. ASSISTED PASSAGES. — WESTERN AUSTRALIA. —

QUEENSLAND.—

No Assisted Passages are given at the present time to CANADA, NEW SOUTH WALES, VICTORIA, SOUTH AUSTRALIA, TASMANIA, NEW ZEALAND, The CAPE or NATAL; but in the case of QUEENSLAND and the CAPE passages at lower rates are given, under special conditions, to Labourers engaged here by employers in those Colonies.

In the case of QUEENSLAND, Land Order Warrants to the value of £20 are given under certain conditions to persons paying their own passage direct to the Colony.

3. NOMINATED PASSAGES. — QUEENSLAND, WESTERN AUSTRALIA, and NATAL.—

QUEENSLAND.—

WESTERN AUSTRALIA.—

NATAL.—£12 per adult.

No Nominated Passages are at present given to CANADA, NEW SOUTH WALES, VICTORIA, SOUTH AUSTRALIA, TASMANIA, NEW ZEALAND, or THE CAPE.

ARRANGEMENTS ON LANDING.

CANADA.—Depôts for emigrants are provided at the ports of Quebec and Halifax and the other principal towns in the Dominion.

NEW SOUTH WALES.—Apply to Mr. G. F. Wise, Immigration Agent, Hyde Park, Sydney.

QUEENSLAND.—

WESTERN AUSTRALIA.—

NEW ZEALAND.—There are Depôts at most of the principal ports for the reception of emigrants.

There are no Government Depôts in VICTORIA, SOUTH AUSTRALIA, TASMANIA, THE CAPE, or NATAL; but there are private agencies in some of these and the other Colonies, particulars of which are given in the Circulars.

BEST TIME FOR ARRIVING.

CANADA.—April to middle of July—not the Winter months.
NEW SOUTH WALES.—Any month—September to November for preference.
VICTORIA.—Ditto.
SOUTH AUSTRALIA.—May to October.
QUEENSLAND.—April to October inclusive.
WESTERN AUSTRALIA.—September to November.
TASMANIA.—Any month—September to November for preference.
NEW ZEALAND.—September to January inclusive.
CAPE.—Any month—August for preference.
NATAL.—Any month—August for preference.

PRESENT DEMAND FOR LABOUR.

FARMERS WITH CAPITAL.—A demand in all the Colonies.
FARM LABOURERS.—A demand for good men in CANADA, NEW SOUTH WALES, VICTORIA, QUEENSLAND, TASMANIA, and some parts of NEW ZEALAND.
MECHANICS AND GENERAL LABOURERS.—
FEMALE DOMESTIC SERVANTS.—

NAMES AND ADDRESSES OF COLONIAL REPRESENTATIVES IN ENGLAND.

CANADA.—High Commissioner, 9, Victoria Chambers, Victoria Street, Westminster, S.W.
NEW SOUTH WALES.—Agent General, 5, Westminster Chambers, Victoria Street, S.W.
VICTORIA.—Agent General, 8, Victoria Chambers, Victoria Street, S.W.
SOUTH AUSTRALIA.—Agent General, 8, Victoria Chambers, Victoria Street, S.W.
QUEENSLAND.—Agent General, 1, Westminster Chambers, Victoria Street, S.W.
WESTERN AUSTRALIA.—The Crown Agents for the Colonies, Downing Street, S.W.
NEW ZEALAND.—Agent General, 7, Westminster Chambers, Victoria Street, S.W.
TASMANIA.—Agent General, 5, Westminster Chambers, Victoria Street, S.W.
CAPE.—Agent General, 7, Albert Mansions, Victoria Street, S.W.
NATAL.—Emigration Agent for Natal, 21, Finsbury Circus, E.C.

Further information can be obtained by writing or personally applying to the Chief Clerk at this office, 31, Broadway, Westminster, S.W., from whom the CIRCULARS issued by the Committee of Management respecting the separate Colonies can be obtained gratis, and the new HANDBOOKS, with Maps and fuller information, at the price of 1d. post free for each Colony.

It is wrong to think that all the people who left Scotland for a new life abroad were poor.

Source 2.18

Marjorie Harper states:

'By no means all emigrants were destitute, disillusioned or hounded out. Many had cash in their pockets as well as well as hope in their hearts, and carried with them a clear plan for the future as well as the means to implement their ideas.'

The lure of more money was a very important reason to leave. Scotland was a low-wage economy and more could be earned overseas. To give one example: in the late nineteenth century it took a granite worker in America one and a half days to earn the same amount of money that it took a week to earn in Scotland. No wonder skilled granite workers in the north-east of Scotland were easy to attract abroad.

Source 2.19

Marjorie Harper sums up the attractions of emigration:

'Scots were lured overseas by a variety of economic, social and cultural inducements. The promise of independence through landownership was a powerful magnet. The artisans produced by Scotland's increasingly urbanised, industrialised society sought higher wages and better working conditions.

For many, the anticipated neighbourliness, cooperation and familiarity of an established Scottish settlement were incentives just as important as material gain and the absence of domineering landlords.'

Such attractions were fed by a correspondence between those Scots who had already emigrated in the years before 1830. The importance of the letter home from a fellow Scot, often a family member, cannot be underestimated. The fact that there was a support network of fellow Scots in existence abroad was an important reason why many emigrated.

Source 2.20

George Mackie, who had settled in New South Wales, Australia, wrote home in 1851:

'Nothing can rejoice a Scotchman's heart more than finding large numbers of them settled all through the district and all doing well. They are principally Highlanders and many of them [if not the whole] who came penniless to the country are now living far more comfortably than many first class farmers in Scotland.'

George Mackie, in his letters home, attacked conditions in Scotland and showed the attractions of colonial life:

Source 2.21

'The Gael is the most industrious, most comfortable man in this colony and also the most willing to work. Such examples as these ought to induce thousands of poor people to emigrate to this colony and ought to disprove those people who, in order to evict the poor highlander, first of all criticise him as an idle, lazy good for nothing fellow.'

The importance of transport

Migration and emigration were also encouraged by cheaper, more efficient transport. By 1850 the building of railways meant that travelling time from Glasgow to London had been reduced to 12 hours. Developments in the technology of steamships meant that a journey time of six weeks for a crossing between Scotland and North America had been reduced to one week by 1914. This reduced journey time for emigrants meant less time not earning money, which was a very important consideration for some people. Interestingly, improvements in technology also encouraged people to return. It has been calculated that up to one third of emigrants returned to Scotland by 1900. The development of railways also meant travel to ports like Glasgow became easier, and allowed for swift movement once within a new country such as Canada or America. Source 2.22 shows how connected transport had become.

Source 2.22

Glasgow and South-Western Railway advertisement

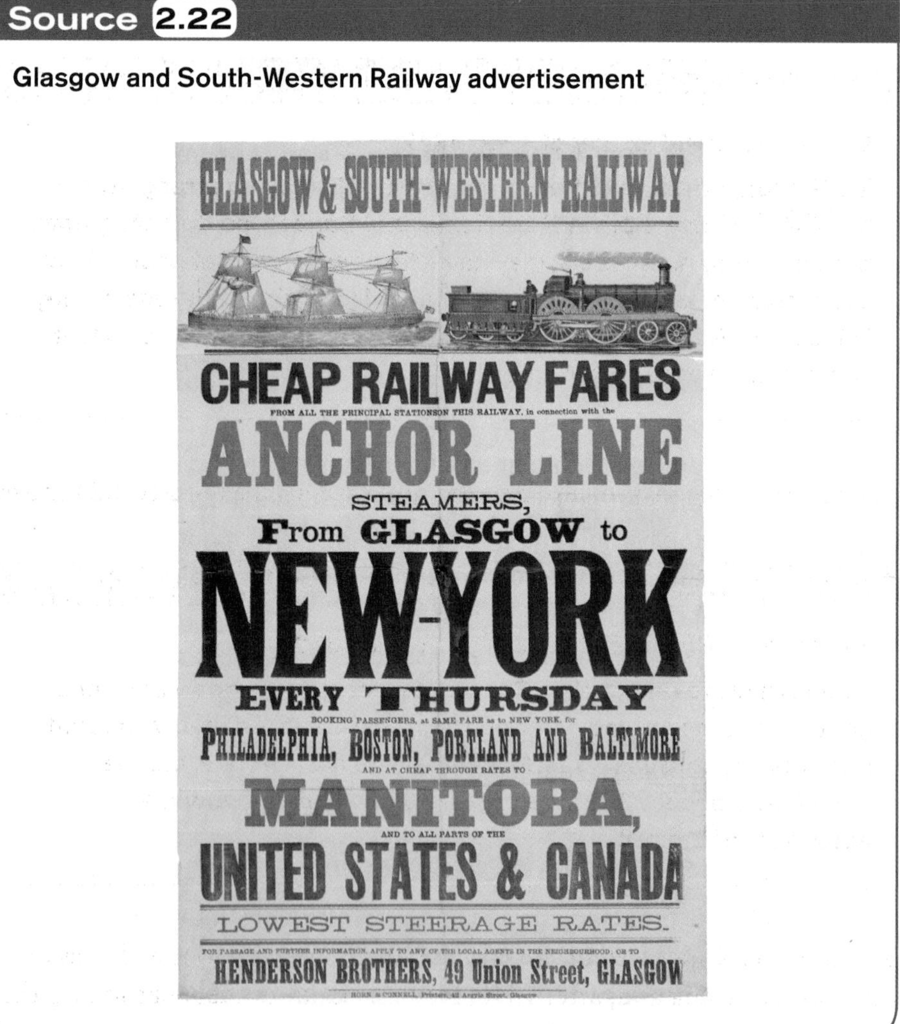

Migration and Empire 1830–1939

Recruiting emigrants

Scots had skills that were attractive to countries such as the United States and Canada. They were excellent farmers and many became very skilled at industrial work such as making ships, railway engines and steam engines. Scots were therefore actively recruited by companies set up to populate and improve the land in places like Canada. In the nineteenth century a network of emigration agencies developed across Scotland. These agencies advertised for passengers and organised their travel arrangements. In 1892 the Canadian Government appointed two full-time agents in Scotland who undertook a tour of markets, hiring fairs, agricultural shows and village halls. In the late nineteenth century Canada, in particular, advertised for workers.

Some agents could also provide land for the emigrant in their destination. John Sutherland was an emigration agent in the Highlands. Source 2.23 gives us a clear picture of the service he offered.

Source 2.23

***Inverness Journal* extract of 1 July 1842:**

'Mr Sutherland, the emigration agent, intends making arrangements for blocks of land, both in Nova Scotia and Canada, so that emigrants, proceeding by his vessels, may have the advantage of at once taking possession of farms or locations without losing their time and money in inquiries. Nearly 2000 emigrants have been sent out by him within two years, in vessels of the first class.'

The press in Scotland provided further encouragement, as Source 2.24 shows.

Source 2.24

Extract from *Chambers' Edinburgh Review* 1872:

'The rewards to emigrate to Canada are not simply good wages and good living among kindred people, under the same flag, in a naturally rich country, possessing a pleasant and healthy climate, but the confident prospect that the poorest may have of becoming a possessor of the soil.'

Similar articles appeared in support of emigration to the United States of America, Australia and, after 1840, New Zealand. Guidebooks to help the emigrant were also produced.

Source 2.25

Nineteenth-century guidebook for emigrants to New Zealand

Help to emigrate

Help was given to encourage emigration by individual landowners, government organisations such as the Colonial Office and charities like the Highlands and Islands Emigration Society.

Emigration societies had developed when unemployed handloom weavers wanted to put pressure on the Government to help them leave Scotland for a better life abroad. Such societies grew as economic problems developed in the Highlands. After the famine of 1846 in Skye, an Emigration Society was set up there in 1851. This developed into the Highlands and Islands Emigration Society. These societies raised money and helped very poor crofters to leave Scotland for Australia and Canada. Emigration was also encouraged by the Government, because they saw it as a safety valve for removing excess population, particularly at times of economic depression. In 1886 the Emigrants' Information Office opened up, giving advice and information on land grants, wages, living costs and passage rates. Overseas governments and land companies also actively advertised the benefits of emigration.

The desire of people to leave, and the attractions of the colonies, are summed up in a news report from the *Inverness Courier* from May 1838.

Source 2.26

Inverness Courier extract:

'After some months of expectation and anxiety, Dr Boyter, the Government emigration agent for Australia, arrived in Fort William. The news of his arrival soon spread through every glen in the district, and at an early hour on the Monday, thousands of enterprising Gaels might be seen ranked around the Caledonian Hotel, anxious to quit the land of their forefathers and go and possess the pastures of Australia. While we regret that so many active men should feel it necessary to leave their own Country, the Highlands will be considerably relieved of this extra population.'

The British Government also provided some help to encourage emigration through the Colonial Land and Emigration Commissioners. This help included giving grants of land in places like Canada and Australia as well as loans of money to help with the costs of passage. However, it was not until the 1922 Empire Settlement Act that the Government became involved in funding emigration to the self-governing dominions directly. This Act committed the British Government to pay up to £3 million a year on a range of policies, including loans and grants to help with passage to the colonies and training courses for emigrants. It was hoped that this would relieve rising unemployment at home, while also binding the Empire more closely together. At a time of economic depression at home it was an astonishing commitment.

Eventually, governments in the colonies directly employed agents. Often they were emigrants themselves. One such example is James Adam, a shipwright from Aberdeen who emigrated to Otago in New Zealand in 1847. Ten years later he returned to Britain as an agent employed by the New Zealand Government. Adam encouraged 4000 Scots to emigrate to New Zealand in the following year. Interestingly 800 of these were related to emigrants who had already settled in New Zealand.

Agents used a number of methods to attract emigrants ranging from giving public talks to private meetings to persuade individuals to emigrate. The New Zealand Government offered free passage to domestic servants, as did the Government of Queensland in Australia in the 1880s. Interestingly this led to complaints from the Canadian Government who felt this was having an effect on their own efforts to attract settlers. Emigrants had to pay for their own fares to Canada at this time. By 1897 the Canadian Government had five agents in Scotland. It had only two agents in England at the same time, showing how important Scotland was as a source of emigrants.

Source 2.27

A 1927 poster advertising for men who wanted to emigrate to Canada. The poster was produced by the Anchor-Donaldson shipping line which was established in Glasgow in 1916, to operate services to Canada. This sort of advert was used to highlight the attraction of jobs and good wages in Canada. The Anchor-Donaldson line sold a lot of one-way tickets to Canda from Scotland in this way.

Summary

Whether it was leaving Scotland to work in England, America or the Empire, the reasons for leaving varied from person to person.

- There were important events such as the Highland Clearances that led people to want to leave Scotland.
- Some Scots were attracted by opportunities such as higher wages and cheap land; others were encouraged by fellow countrymen who had already moved.
- Scots were attractive workers because of their skills and the fact that many brought money with them.
- Countries like Canada put considerable effort into attracting Scots through agents, posters and other advertising.
- Quicker and more affordable travel was also a factor encouraging people to leave. Scots developed a system of supporting each other when abroad, which led to an increased sense of their Scottish identity.

Source 2.28

Historian Christopher Smout states:

'It is often asked about migration whether the pull factors are more important than push factors; it is never easy to give a clear-cut answer, because the choice of every individual depends on his preferences and on his personal estimate of the advantages of going or staying. A pull from the cities, always attractive to the adventurous, might become compulsive to many more as their opportunities became better known and the opportunities at home narrowed, or the way of life the country offered seemed less and less to be the only way of life possible.'

Activities 

Your target is to teach a lesson, in groups of three or four, to the rest of your class about ONE of the three following issues.

- What were the reasons for the internal migration of Scots?
- What were the opportunities that attracted Scots to move to other countries?
- What were the factors that forced Scots to leave their country?

Your main resource for information is this textbook. You must also access other resources to help you answer your issue.

Planning

- You will need to negotiate with your teacher about how much time you will have to complete this task.
- As a class you will decide on the criteria for a successful lesson.
- Your lesson should be as interesting, colourful and interactive as you can make it. (Obviously this will depend on what resources there are in your classroom.)
- All members of the groups must be involved in the preparation, research and delivery of the lesson.

The lesson

- Think carefully about what you want your classmates to do during the lesson.
- It is important that they do more than just listen to your group talking. They will need activities to complete, and they will need notes on your subject. You might also want them to practise a skill like a source-based question.
- Remember the criteria you have previously agreed about your lesson.

Evaluation

- You will all have a chance to comment on the lesson once it has been completed. Use the criteria you have previously agreed in order to see if you have been successful. What went well? What could be worked on in the future?

The experience of immigrants in Scotland

Scotland's developing economy had a need for workers. The migration of people from the countryside to the towns provided much of the workforce. However, another source of labour came from people who left their own country to work in Scotland. The experience of these immigrants in Scotland differed according to their religion as well as the jobs they did.

By 1830, Scotland had a real sense of its own identity in terms of religion, language and culture. Immigrants who worshipped a different religion or spoke a different language were viewed with suspicion. Some were even thought to threaten the 'Scottish' way of life. However, as time went on, some groups were accepted, while others developed separate systems and structures that reinforced their own sense of identity.

Irish immigration

In 1830, Ireland had a growing population but it was badly affected by poverty. At that time, the whole of Ireland was part of the United Kingdom, so many Irish workers simply made the short sea-crossing to Scotland to help with lifting potatoes or other seasonal work, only to return home once the season had passed. As the industrial economy of Scotland developed so did the demand for unskilled and semi-skilled labour. Jobs emerged building the railways and canals that would provide the transport routes for industry. Pay was high compared with wages at home so many Irish immigrants filled these jobs.

Source 3.1

A present day map showing Ireland's proximity to Scotland

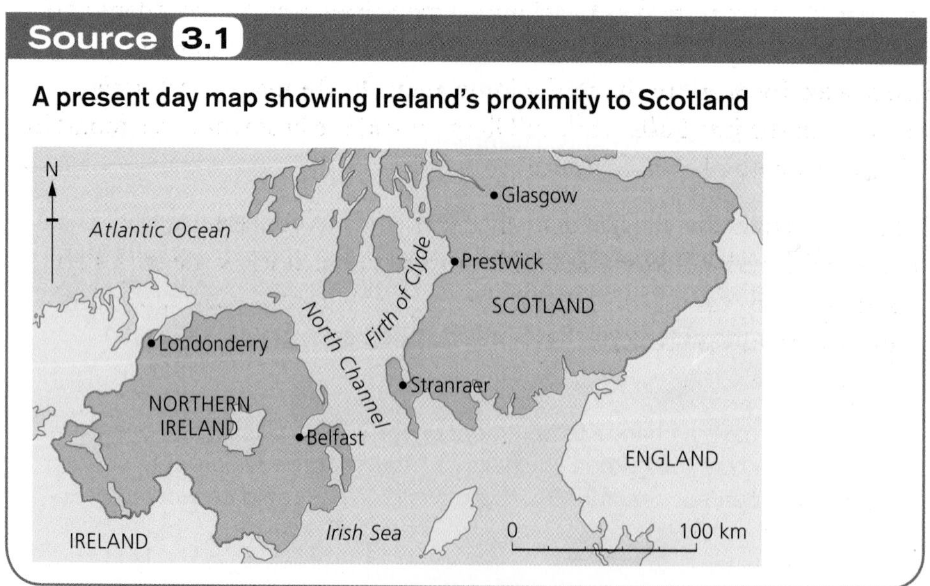

Migration and hunger

The Census of 1841 counts 125,000 Irish-born citizens living in Scotland. By 1851 Irish immigrants made up 7.2 per cent of the population of Scotland. In comparison, Irish immigrants made up only 2.1 per cent of England's population at this time.

The Irish Potato Famine of 1845–51 caused a huge increase in Irish migration. Over one million Irish died because of hunger and disease. A million more emigrated. Although places like America attracted larger numbers of Irish, the impact of Irish immigration to Scotland was of huge importance.

The Catholic Irish experience

The difficulties experienced by Catholic Irish immigrants in the Lowlands of Scotland were similar to those of the migrant Highlander. Most immigrant Irish spoke a different language and practised a different religion.

Scotland in 1830 was a Protestant country. Figures show that in the 1780s, before the arrival of the Irish, there were approximately 30,000 Catholics out of a total population of 1.5 million. These were mostly in the west Highlands and islands or the north-east.

The first Irish immigrants seem to have integrated well with the native Scots despite being mostly Catholic. Many changed their surnames to integrate with the Scots, intermarried and even converted to Protestantism. If there was any conflict linked with the Irish immigrants at that time it tended to be between the Catholic 'Green' Irish and the Protestant 'Orange' Irish rather than between Irish and Scots.

Growing resentment

The number of poor Catholic Irish flooding into Scotland led to a growing resentment among Scots. The Irish were very visible as they tended to concentrate in areas such as the slums of the Saltmarket, Cowcaddens and Maryhill in Glasgow or the Lochee area of Dundee. In the Lothians the Irish looked for work in the coal mining areas. In Dundee the attraction was work in the jute mills while in Glasgow and the best work was found in the increasing number of factories.

The problem of Irish immigration into Britain was a concern for the Government, and a Commission of Inquiry into the State of the Irish Poor in Great Britain was set up in 1835. The Inquiry's general view of the Irish is summed up in Source 3.2.

Source 3.2

Extract from the Commission of Inquiry into the State of the Irish Poor in Great Britain, produced in 1836:

'The general character of the Irish immigration into Great Britain is that persons for whom there is little or no demand in their own country seek employment in England or Scotland at a rate of wages somewhat lower than that paid to the lowest paid local labourers. The kind of work at which they are employed is usually of the roughest and most repulsive description, and requiring the least skill. Their way of life is similar to that of the poorest of the native population, if not inferior to it.'

Many immigrants were poor. They were easy to blame for the problems caused by urbanisation, as Source 3.3 shows.

Source 3.3

Extract from the Commission of Inquiry into the State of the Irish Poor in Great Britain, produced in 1836:

'The Irish are, in general, dirtier and less well clothed than the native population. In consequence of the crowded nature of the Irish lodging houses, typhus is more common among the Irish in Glasgow than among the Scotch. Generally speaking we find that in housing, comfort, education and moral feeling, the Irish are inferior to the Scotch.'

Christopher Smout points out why the jobs the Irish Catholics did also led to them gaining a bad reputation.

Source 3.4

Historian Christopher Smout states:

'For the unskilled on low or irregular wages it was much more difficult to keep up a respectable lifestyle however hard you saved. It was so much more tempting to blow everything on a hard night's drinking or bet on a horse when there was a chance of winning money. Consequently labourers, and the Irish in particular, came to have a reputation for fighting, drunkenness and general "bad" behaviour. It was easy for the middle classes to retain the comforting belief that the Irish poor remained poor because they were morally bad.'

Stories spread that the Irish came to Scotland to get access to the help available to the poor that existed at the time. This help was called Poor Relief and could be claimed after three years living in Scotland. In this sense the Irish were looked at as the equivalent of today's 'benefit scrounger'.

The poem in Source 3.5 was written in 1858 by a Poor Law Inspector. It suggests that the Scots were being taken for fools by the cunning Irish.

Source 3.5

THE IRISH PAUPER IN IRELAND TO HIS NEIGHBOURS

Och! Come from the West boys, come hook it with me;
'Tis a dirty ould peat bog polluting the sea,
Where black hunger grins from each mud cabin door;
Then come where there's parties and whisky galore,
They'll feed us, and clothe us, with all the best,
And make us their own though we come from the West.
In the poorhouse of Scotland we'll live at our ease;
It's no more like our Unions than peats are like paise;
For here work and starvation is always the test,
Then why stay any longer in this Bog of the West?
But come from the West and in Scotland you'll find
Lots of grub, without work, and faith that's to your mind.

Irish workers were also accused of being strike-breakers and being willing to work for less money than Scottish workers.

Organisations emerged in Scotland to oppose the Irish Catholic community. Such organisations emphasised the Protestant nature of Scotland and suggested that the Irish Catholics were a threat. They were accused of following a different leader in the 'Pope' and of having no loyalty to Scotland as a result. One Protestant organisation, the Scottish Reformation Society, was founded in 1850 and was supported by publications such as *The Bulwark* and *The Scottish Protestant.*

Source 3.6

Front cover of *The Bulwark*, the official magazine of the Scottish Reformation Society

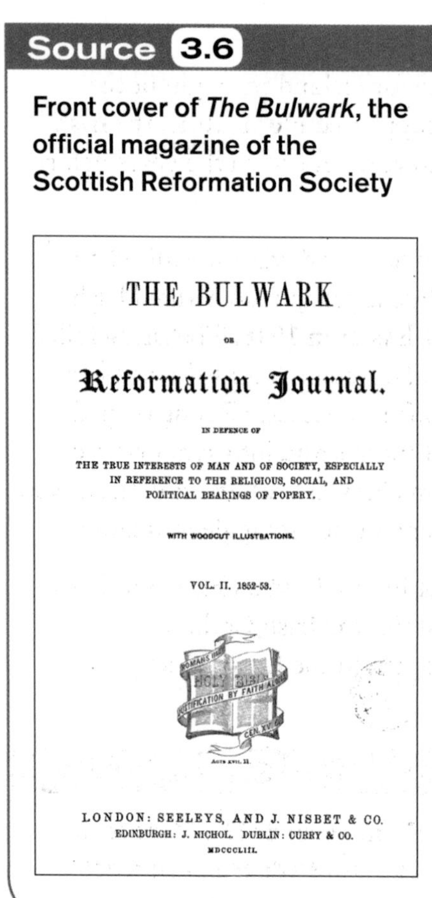

THE BULWARK

OR

Reformation Journal.

IN DEFENCE OF

THE TRUE INTERESTS OF MAN AND OF SOCIETY, ESPECIALLY IN REFERENCE TO THE RELIGIOUS, SOCIAL, AND POLITICAL BEARINGS OF POPERY.

WITH WOODCUT ILLUSTRATIONS.

VOL. II. 1852-53.

LONDON: SEELEYS, AND J. NISBET & CO.
EDINBURGH: J. NICHOL. DUBLIN: CURRY & CO.
MDCCCLIII.

Catholic identity

With the increase in immigration from Ireland, the Catholic Church expanded its services in Scotland. In Glasgow alone the number of priests increased from 134 in 1878 to 234 by 1902. The Church was a place of safety, security and identity for many Irish immigrants, especially when they faced hostility from the local Protestant population.

Organisations such as the League of the Cross were set up to combat the evils of alcohol. Intermarriage between Catholics and non-Catholics became difficult as young Catholic men and women were encouraged to socialise together in halls attached to Chapels. Even a separate sporting identity was created with the emergence of Edinburgh Hibernian in 1873 and Celtic football club in 1888.

Catholic schools also developed in this period, but they were funded by voluntary donations. Given the poverty of most Catholic Irish this was a remarkable achievement. It was not until 1918 that Catholic schools received funding from the Government. The Education (Scotland) Act 1918 allowed Catholic schools into the state system funded through education rates. It also gave the schools the right to give Catholic religious instruction and select their own teachers. This was to prove very controversial. Protestant groups argued that their local taxation (rates) should not be used to pay for Catholic schools. Their slogan was 'No Rome on the Rates!'. The argument even led to the emergence of a political party.

The Scottish Protestant League was a political party in Scotland during the 1920s and 1930s that wanted to repeal the Education Act. It also wanted to stop Irish immigration to Britain, repatriate Irish immigrants already settled and deport Irish immigrants who were on welfare benefits. The party had some minor success in electing three councillors in Glasgow, but it fizzled out after 1934, although its newspaper, *The Vanguard*, survived until 1939.

The Irish and politics

Most Catholic Irish supported Home Rule for Ireland throughout the nineteenth century. As the Liberal Party supported Home Rule, the Irish Catholic community in Scotland tended to vote Liberal in the years before the First World War.

However, the Catholic Irish community in Scotland was radicalised by events in Dublin in 1916. Sinn Fein, a political group who wanted Irish independence, staged a rising in Dublin at Easter in 1916. The rising failed. The British Government then captured and executed Sinn Fein members. The brutality of British troops in Ireland after the Easter Rising turned many Irish living in Scotland against the Liberals and into supporters of Sinn Fein. By 1920 there were 80 Sinn Fein clubs in Scotland and these were a significant source of finance for the independence struggle in Ireland.

Although support for Sinn Fein fizzled out in 1922, when Eire (Southern Ireland) was given independence from Britain, the Irish Catholic community in Scotland had moved its support to the Labour Party.

Sectarianism

Economic troubles were frequently at the root of tension between Scots and Irish. In the 1840s and 1850s the poor Irish immigrant could be seen as a drain on the Scots. Similarly, in the 1920s and 1930s, as economic depression hit Scotland after the war, Scots looked to the Irish as scapegoats. The 1920s saw widespread violence between Catholic and Protestant communities. In this climate the Church of Scotland published its famous pamphlet 'The Menace of the Irish Race to our Scottish Identity' in 1923. Such publications showed that strong anti-Irish Catholic feelings remained in Scotland.

Source 3.7

Front cover of *The Menace of the Irish Race to our Scottish Identity* pamphlet

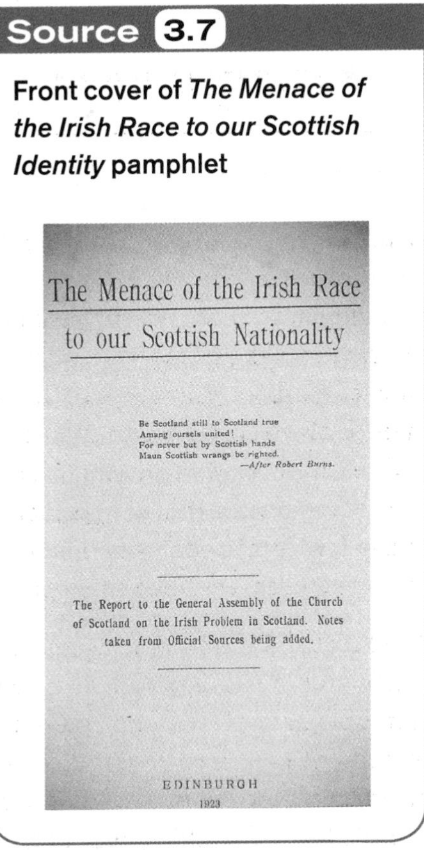

The Menace of the Irish Race to our Scottish Nationality

Be Scotland still to Scotland true
Amang oursels united!
For never but by Scottish hands
Maun Scottish wrangs be righted.
—*After Robert Burns.*

The Report to the General Assembly of the Church of Scotland on the Irish Problem in Scotland. Notes taken from Official Sources being added.

EDINBURGH
1923

Co-operation

It would, however, be wrong to paint the experience of the Catholic Irish in Scotland as one of constant conflict with the Scottish community. The Catholic Irish had a shared experience with the Scottish worker in that

they were both affected by industrialisation and urbanisation, and they fought together during the First World War. In fact, any argument that the Catholic Irish had no loyalty to the British state was effectively ended during the Great War when Catholic Irish volunteered and fought for the British state, dying in large numbers.

The historian Martin Mitchell has pointed out that there was considerable co-operation between Irish Catholics and fellow Scottish working class in the trade union movement as well as the temperance movement. From the 1870s onwards Irish miners from both Protestant and Catholic communities were important as members and leaders of the Lanarkshire Miners' Union for example. Irish Catholics were also important in the National Iron and Steelworkers Union and joined industrial disputes with their fellow workers.

The temperance movement thought that alcohol use was bad and should be stopped. They stood for what is known as teetotalism, which means living your life without using alcohol. The Irish Catholic and Scottish Protestant communities worked together to promote this. One example of this co-operation can be seen in July 1841 when a march of over 5000 Catholic and Protestant 'teetotalers' took place through Glasgow.

The Protestant Irish experience

About one in four Irish immigrants were Protestants. The Irish Protestant had a lot in common with the average Scot (see Source 3.8).

Source 3.8

Historian Graham Walker states:

'Many lowland Scots, especially in the South-West of the country, looked upon Ulster as an extension of the way of life of their region. Presbyterianism (the Scottish form of the Protestant church) provided the basic common ground as well as, of course, the large amount of family and ancestral connections. Cultural interaction between Ulster and lowland Scotland went deep.'

Irish Protestants had been coming over to Scotland in large numbers since the eighteenth century. Their skills as weavers and in bleaching cloth meant they were in demand. This movement was originally a temporary migration, with the workers returning to Ireland once their work was done. However, as wages increased in Scotland and the linen industry declined in Ireland, many Irish Protestants settled in Scotland. Given their skills, many of the Irish Protestants settled in areas where the weaving trade was strong, such as Renfrewshire, Ayrshire and Glasgow. They also worked as rural labourers in the south-west of Scotland.

Issues of identity

There are two areas of life in which the Protestant Irish made a very distinctive impact on Scotland. The first is through the Orange Lodge (or Orange Order), a Protestant organisation. The 'Orange' movement was started in Ulster in 1795. It was a Protestant reaction against Catholic secret societies that wanted to get rid of Protestants in Ireland at that time. The first Scottish lodge opened in 1800 in the weaving centre of Maybole in Ayrshire. The growth of the lodge system in Scotland shows the spread of Irish Protestantism, at least until the 1850s. By 1835 there were 12 lodges in Glasgow as well as two in Paisley and numerous others in the south-west and Edinburgh. The historian Graham Walker sums up importance of the Orange Order (Source 3.9).

Source 3.9

Graham Walker states:

'Orange Order membership seems to have been viewed by Protestant immigrants as a way of maintaining a distinct identity, of distinguishing themselves from the Catholic Irish.'

The disagreements fought out between Protestant 'Orange' and Catholic 'Green' in Ireland was therefore transported into Scotland. Sectarian trouble between the two communities existed in Glasgow, Ayrshire and Lanarkshire in the 1830s. With the development of the coal industry in Scotland such conflicts spread to Stirlingshire, Dunbartonshire and the Lothians.

Source 3.10

The Orange Order uses symbols and images of historic Protestant victories over Catholics, like this portrait of King William of Orange.

The second major effect of Irish Protestant migration to Scotland was their prominence in skilled industries such as shipbuilding and the iron industry. Firms like Bairds of Coatbridge employed mainly Protestant Irish. They advertised their job vacancies in Belfast, gave their workers houses and provided education for the workers' children. Areas such as Larkhall in Lanarkshire also developed a distinct 'Orange' identity. This was reinforced by further immigration from the Northern Irish counties as the nineteenth century progressed. Irish Protestants remained important in the Orange Order at this time.

It would be wrong to think of the Protestant Irish as being more skilled than their Catholic counterparts. However, areas of distinct Irish Protestant economic dominance certainly developed. This was particularly true in shipbuilding.

Source 3.11

Historian Christopher Smout comments:

'The foreman, indeed, had great powers of hiring and firing. In many Clyde engineering works and shipyards – most famously in John Browns – they were Freemasons, Orangemen and Rangers supporters who thought it part of their calling to discourage the Catholic Irish. The sectarian balance at work was definitely on the Protestant side. It took a long time before being Catholic ceased to mean being at the bottom of the pile in most manufacturing employments.'

Source 3.12

Historian Graham Walker comments:

'We can be sure of their presence in the Orange Order and, after around 1890, of the support of many of them for the Govan-based Rangers football club which was already emerging as the Protestant answer to the proudly Irish and Catholic Celtic.

Both inside Glasgow and in these nearby towns the Protestant Irish seem to have adapted to the labour and employment characteristics of the area. For example, they were well represented in the high quality skilled textile work of Paisley, and in the unskilled, casual work of Greenock. They were also a significant part of the mining and heavy industrial workforce in Ayrshire and Lanarkshire, and to a lesser extent Dunbartonshire, Stirlingshire and West Lothian.'

The Protestant Irish and politics

Protestants supported the Union of Ireland with England and Scotland, so they opposed moves to Irish Home Rule in the years before 1914. The Conservatives supported the Union so the Orange movement gave its support to the Conservatives. As a result the Conservatives had considerable working-class support among the skilled working classes in the central belt of Scotland. When much of Ireland became independent after 1922 the issue that so divided Orange and Green in Scotland had largely gone. Indeed, Christopher Smout states 'the absorption of the Irish into the social fabric of Scottish life must be considered one of the achievements of Scottish history'. However, in one important and long-lasting way, the Protestant/Catholic division did not go away.

Source 3.13

Historian Christopher Smout comments:

'In the 1920s and 1930s, at least in Glasgow, football violence increased in sectarian content as Celtic began to fly the Irish Free State flag at its matches and Rangers flaunted its Union Jacks and orange supporters' badges in response. Club management arguably encouraged sectarianism and its accompanying violence as a crowd-puller, so that it became part of the ritual pattern of Glasgow male recreation.'

Jews

In 1860 it was estimated that only 26 Jewish families lived in Glasgow. The community was small but successful, and many Jews lived in the fashionable West End of Glasgow. Things were to change in the later nineteenth century.

Large numbers of Jews arrived between 1880 and 1914. This was part of a much larger movement of Jewish people, mostly from Eastern Europe. These Jews were different from those who had settled in the wealthy West End of Glasgow. Most of the newcomers were poor and came from Russia and Poland. They were fleeing from religious and economic persecution. The opportunity to leave their countries of origin had also improved because of the increasing availability of fast and reasonably cheap travel.

Most of the Jews from Eastern Europe were escaping from pogroms (a pogrom is an organised massacre of a particular ethnic group) in the Russian Empire. One estimate calculates that the population of Russian Jews in Scotland was around 6000 in 1903 and by 1919 over 9000 lived in Glasgow alone. Most lived in the Gorbals area, which offered cheap lodgings, and enabled these Jews to live alongside other Jews who spoke Yiddish, the main Jewish language at that time.

The Jewish population developed into a community and built synagogues to worship in, such as one built in South Portland Street in Glasgow at a cost of £9000. Jewish reading rooms were set up, and a Benevolent Loan Society. In 1901 nearly 200 loans were granted to Jewish businesses. Jewish immigrants tended to work in particular jobs such as peddling and hawking (selling door to door).

Source 3.14

Scottish Jew Ralph Glasser remembers:

'These loans were granted free from interest mainly to pedlars and travellers and that gave them the basis for making a living from the stock that they could buy and sell. They were selling various things, braces, mouth-organs, games, small things that needed small money for stock. When they became a little wealthier they paid the money back.'

Source 3.15

Another Scottish Jew, Mrs Aitken, remembers:

'It was nearly all Jewish shops and firms in the Gorbals. There was the Fogels, the corner of Hospital Street and Cleland Street, there was the Jewish bakery at the corner of Dunmore Street. Gleicken, the gown people were there and the Ashers as well. The Gerbers, the Woolfsons, them that had all the jewellers, the shops in the Trongate, they came from there. There were small cabinet-making businesses and upholstery work right up to Cumberland Street. They all opened little shops, just doing alterations and repairs to suits and everything. It was a great place the Gorbals.'

Jews and the sweated trades

It was not long before Scottish trade unions complained about Jews undercutting wages. The unions also complained about the so-called 'sweated trades'. Sweated trades describe those trades that paid very low wages and forced their workers to work long hours. In doing so they undercut skilled workers' wages. Sweated labour was mainly associated with Jewish immigrants (see Source 3.16).

Source 3.16

A tailor's trade union leader claimed to the 1889 House of Lords Select Committee on Sweating:

'The wholesale sweaters in Glasgow are chiefly Jews and the number is said to be increasing, though on this point evidence is somewhat scanty. It is computed that the workers in the tailoring trade in Glasgow number about 5000 or 6000.'

Although further evidence noted that a large proportion of the sweaters were Scottish and Irish, those on the ground saw the problem as an immigrant problem, and in Glasgow that meant a Jewish problem.

Source 3.17

Jewish workers in a cap factory in Glasgow

Resentment of Jews

Trade unions were understandably against sweated labour as it affected the wages of their members. As resentment of Jewish immigrants grew, newspapers also became involved, reporting that Britain was an easy country to get into and had become a dumping ground for undesirables. *The Daily Record and Mail* in the west of Scotland in August 1905 featured the heading 'Alien danger: Immigrants infected with loathsome disease'. Many Jews who had been resident in Britain for some time and had integrated into the local population also felt that the new community of poor Jews threatened to alienate the local population, encouraging anti-semitic behaviour.

However, help was available for the poorer Jews from within the Jewish community itself. The Glasgow Jewish Board of Guardians and the Hebrew Ladies' Benevolent Society in 1901 were dealing with 500 cases of needy Jews. Very few Jews received any help from local poor relief.

This contradicted the accusation made by many that the Jewish population were a burden. Yet the large number of poorer Jews arriving in Scotland did create racial tension. Jews in Scotland faced prejudice and discrimination from the local population; they were attacked for their religion. Having a Jewish surname could even affect prospects when looking for lodgings. Source 3.18 describes a stereotypical view of Jews at that time.

Source 3.18

In 1893 J.A. Hammerton described his image of a Jew in *Sketches from Glasgow*:

'He has a rather sallow complexion, and his face is fringed with straggling black whiskers. He wears a frock coat that was black long ago. A glance at him is sufficient to proclaim him a son of Israel. He is a money lender in the city – like not a few of his tribe.'

Yet the Jewish population also integrated (see Source 3.19).

Source 3.19

Historian Murdoch Rodgers sums up the life of the Jew in Scotland:
'It was possibly because they shared in the poverty that surrounded them that there was, by all accounts, little active opposition to the Jews at street or tenement close level. Communal relations appear to have been little different to those experienced by other "foreigners", whether from Ireland, Italy, Lithuania or Edinburgh. The immigrant Jews in fact lived a fairly self-contained and independent existence, well organised but poor, tolerated but not accepted.

Indeed, although there was anti-semitism among the local population, it was never widespread, and the Jewish community thrived.

Source 3.20

Scottish Jewish commentator Kenneth Collins states:

'Certainly, compared to their experiences in Eastern Europe the Jews found Glasgow tolerant and easy going, a city which provided them with economic opportunities and gave their children a framework for education which would transform the financial and social base of the community. Furthermore anti-semitism was a disreputable attitude in British society. Glasgow Jewry never numbered more than 15,000 at its peak during the interwar period and one can speculate that the limits of tolerance might have been different had the numbers of Jews settling in the city been much higher. The onward movement of Jewish migrants to America kept the Jewish population of the city at a level which the local community could safely accommodate.'

Some identities were also more important than being a Jewish (see Source 3.21).

Source 3.21

Scottish Jew Mrs Woofson remembers:

'When I was at school I was challenged by one of my friends and I was asked whether I was a Protestant or a Catholic and I said, 'No, I'm a Jew.' So I was then asked whether I was a Protestant Jew or a Catholic Jew. Well, I went to a Protestant school so I said, 'I'm a Protestant Jew!'

By the 1920s and 1930s the distinct Jewish identity was disappearing as the Jews integrated more and more with the local population of Scotland. The Yiddish language began to die out, as did Yiddish newspapers. Jewish supporters of Rangers and Celtic were to be found on the terraces of Ibrox and Parkhead. The Jew in Scotland had become a Scottish Jew.

Lithuanians

Another group of immigrants who passed through Scotland on their way to America were Lithuanians. Lithuanians fled from Eastern Europe for reasons similar to those of the Jews. It was not only Jews who felt the effects of persecution in Eastern Europe. It has been calculated that between 1868 and 1914 approximately 25 per cent of the Lithuanian population decided to move from their homeland in an attempt to escape persecution, high taxation and falling incomes. About 7000 Lithuanians decided to settle in Scotland.

Scotland had attractions for poor Lithuanians in need of some cash. For a start there were jobs in the growing industries of coal, iron and steel in Lanarkshire and Ayrshire. Employment also came with accommodation in many of these industries. In addition, stopping in Scotland and then sailing from Glasgow or Leith to America was cheaper than travelling direct to America.

At first local workers disliked the new immigrants.

Source 3.22

Historian Murdoch Rodgers states:

'The sudden emergence of "colonies" of Lithuanian settlement provoked considerable local opposition. As early as 1887 the Ayrshire Miners Union led by Keir Hardie demanded their removal on the grounds that "their presence is a menace to the health and morality of the place and is, besides, being used to reduce the already too low wages earned by the workmen". ...The powerful Lanarkshire County Miners' Union (LCMU), for example, focused attention on the threat to employment and safety which the Lithuanian miners posed and offered official backing to a number of strikes protesting against their presence in the mines.'

Most Scottish complaints about the Lithuanians being dirty, barbarous and immoral had no real substance, but at first the Lithuanian workers were used to break pit disputes in the mining industry. They would work when the union was on strike, for example. However, in time the Lithuanians worked with the local miners and joined the strikes themselves to improve working conditions in the mines. This was largely supported by Lithuanian newspapers that emerged at this time. The local trade unions further helped integration by encouraging Lithuanian membership.

In reality it was difficult to tell how many Lithuanians were working in the mines. One clever and simple way in which the Lithuanians integrated into the local population was to change their surnames: Lithuanian names Bernotaitis, Sharmaitis and Vilcinskis became Brown, Smith and Miller.

Source 3.23

Lithuanian coal miners in Bellshill

Lithuanian identity in Scotland

To begin with the Lithuanians maintained a distinct sense of identity. There were separate Lithuanian newspapers called *Vaidelyte* (Vestel) and then *Laikas* (Time), Lithuanian shops and even Lithuanian insurance societies.

Source 3.24

A Lithuanian information pamphlet from 1902. Such pamphlets offered advice to Lithuanians in Scotland. This one is offering services such as translation of papers and documents.

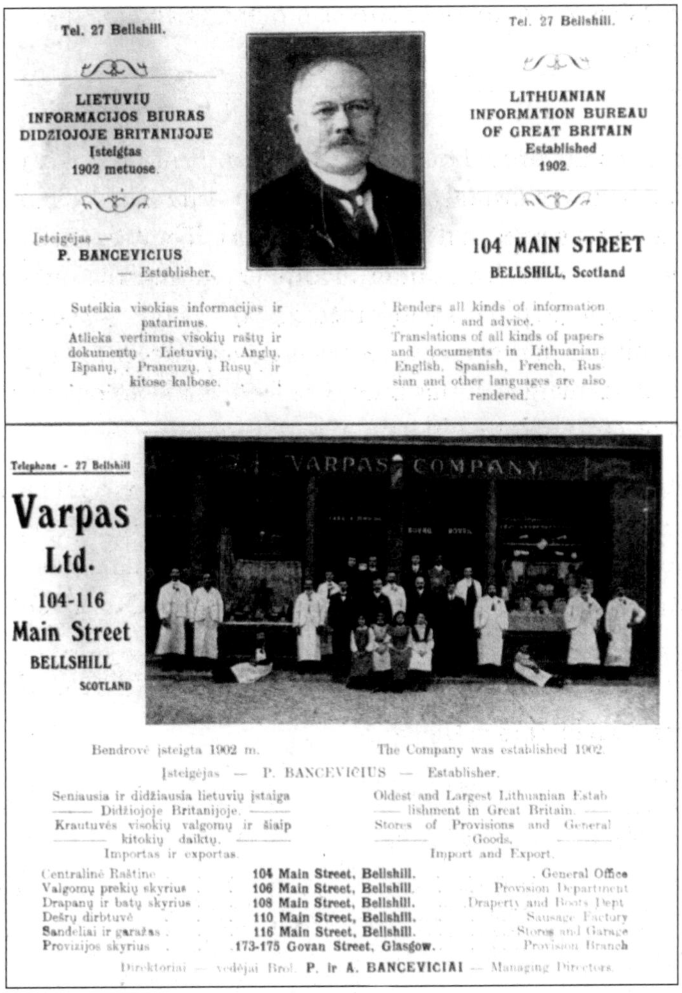

Tel. 27 Bellshill.

LIETUVIŲ
INFORMACIJOS BIURAS
DIDŽIOJOJE BRITANIJOJE
Įsteigtas
1902 metuose.

Įsteigėjas —
P. BANCEVICIUS
— Establisher.

Suteikia visokias informacijas ir patarimus.
Atlieka vertimus visokių raštų ir dokumentų. Lietuvių, Anglų, Išpanų, Prancuzų, Rusų ir kitose kalbose.

Tel. 27 Bellshill.

LITHUANIAN
INFORMATION BUREAU
OF GREAT BRITAIN
Established
1902.

104 MAIN STREET
BELLSHILL, Scotland

Renders all kinds of information and advice.
Translations of all kinds of papers and documents in Lithuanian, English, Spanish, French, Russian and other languages are also rendered.

Telephone - 27 Bellshill

Varpas Ltd.

104-116
Main Street
BELLSHILL
SCOTLAND

VARPAS COMPANY

Bendrovė įsteigta 1902 m. — The Company was established 1902.

Įsteigėjas — P. BANCEVICIUS — Establisher.

Seniausia ir didžiausia lietuvių įstaiga Didžiojoje Britanijoje. — Oldest and Largest Lithuanian Establishment in Great Britain.
Krautuvės visokių valgomų ir šiaip kitokių daiktų. — Stores of Provisions and General Goods.
Importas ir exportas. — Import and Export.

Centralinė Raštinė	104 Main Street, Bellshill.	General Office
Valgomų prekių skyrius	106 Main Street, Bellshill.	Provision Department
Drapanų ir batų skyrius	108 Main Street, Bellshill.	Drapery and Boots Dept.
Dešrų dirbtuvė	110 Main Street, Bellshill.	Sausage Factory
Sandeliai ir garažas	116 Main Street, Bellshill.	Stores and Garage
Provizijos skyrius	173-175 Govan Street, Glasgow.	Provision Branch

Direktoriai — vedėjai Brol. P. ir A. BANCEVICIAI — Managing Directors.

These reminders of home helped many Lithuanians cope with the difficulties of settling in a new land.

Source 3.25

Author Murdoch Rodgers comments:

'The immigrant community could claim a fair measure of success in providing a specifically Lithuanian alternative to local culture and custom. This was perhaps less important to the males in the community who were in regular contact with fellow workers who were not Lithuanian but to the Lithuanian women it provided a lifeline which helped to offset the feelings of isolation after arrival. It goes some way to explaining why so few of the Lithuanian women of the first generation of settlement learned to speak English. It was simply not necessary.'

The effect of the First World War

The First World War had huge consequences for the Lithuanian community in Scotland. On 6 July 1917 the Anglo-Russian Military Convention was signed. It stated that all Russian males (Lithuanians were considered to be Russian as their country was part of the Russian Empire) aged between 18 and 41 resident in Britain faced the choice of conscription into the British Army or deportation for military service in Russia. This split the Lithuanian community. Lithuanian priests supported the view that joining the British Army was the better option. The local Lithuanian Socialists wanted men to return to Russia to help work for the revolution that was brewing in Russia. Of the 1800 Lithuanians who were called up, 700 joined the British Army and 1100 chose to be deported to Russia. The more radical and anti-war Lithuanians opposed this conscription totally.

The Russian revolution took place at the end of 1917. Under Lenin, the Communists seized power, and many countries, including Britain, feared that a communist revolution could spread across Europe. The British Government saw the Lithuanian community as a possible communist threat and was keen to see them removed from the country.

In 1920 the UK Government withdrew financial allowances for Lithuanian women and children whose menfolk had not returned from Russia to Scotland. As a result 600 Lithuanian women and children returned to Russian soil. This loss of young men and women meant that the ability of the Lithuanians to keep a distinctive identity was slowly lost, and the presence of a thriving Lithuanian community in Scotland became a fading memory.

Italians

Although Italians have lived in Scotland for many years they did not settle here in large numbers until after 1880. By 1914 the Italian community in Scotland numbered approximately 4500. The Italian community thrived in

Scotland because Italians provided two things that became hugely popular to Scots: ice-cream and fish and chips.

Most of the Italians who settled in Scotland originated from two areas of Italy: the little Tuscan hilltop town of Barga and its surrounding countryside in the province of Lucca, and the towns of Filignano and Picinisco south of Rome.

Source 3.26

Scottish–Italian author Joe Pieri states:

'In the early part of the twentieth century scarcely a family could be found in these two areas which did not have a relative running either a fish and chip shop or an ice-cream parlour somewhere in Scotland.'

To begin with, Italian immigrants sold ice-cream from barrows and were called 'Hokey Pokey' men from their street cry of '*Ecco un pocco*'. As the business grew this developed into shops and even chains of cafes.

Source 3.27

Ice-cream barrow in Dundee, 1907

The presence of these businesses was not always welcomed by the Scottish population. Chief amongst the criticisms was the fact that many cafes, ice-cream shops and fish and chip shops were open on a Sunday. To the God-fearing, church-going Scot this was unacceptable. The basic objection

seems to have been that these were places where men and women could meet and socialise freely. However, other Scots supported these businesses because they provided an alternative to the public house and the temptations of alcohol.

Issues of identity

Italians settling in Scotland often intended to work for a while to raise money and then return home to Italy. This, and the long hours of work in the cafes and fish and chip shops, meant that they did not always integrate with the local Scottish population. The Italians were generally welcomed by the Scots as they were not seen as a threat to local Scots' jobs or wages, but they remained a separate community. Many Scots called the Italians 'Tallies'.

Source 3.28

Joe Pieri remembers:

'The counter between myself and our customers acted as a barrier. We were aliens, foreigners, the Tallies who worked all day to serve them fish and chips and ice-cream, and we were tolerated as such.'

This sense of separation is commented on by historian Tom Devine.

Source 3.29

Tom Devine states:

'Italian was spoken at home, food was in the Italian style, children were expected to marry Italians and strong parental control ensured that they did so throughout the 1920s, 1930s and beyond. The social life of the girls of the family was especially restricted. Most time was spent in the shops because of the long working hours, and the room behind the shop counter became the meeting points for friends and relatives. For many the hope, and for some the reality, was eventually to return to Italy, and therefore any attempt at assimilation into Scottish society seemed pointless.'

This sense of separation was reinforced by the development of Italian clubs. When Mussolini became fascist dictator of Italy in 1922 he was aware of the fact that many of the youngest, brightest and best left Italy to better themselves, mostly in America, but also in places like Scotland. He was aware that this was a resource he could use and this led to the development of fascist clubs for Italian emigrants to retain an affinity with Italy. La Casa

del Fascio established itself in Glasgow and provided a focus for the Scottish Italian community. With the outbreak of war in 1939, particularly after Mussolini declared war on Britain in 1940, these clubs, and Italian shops and businesses, were attacked. After the war the Casa del Fascio became known as Casa d'Italia and was a place to meet and socialise as well as encourage a love of Italian language and culture. Branches emerged in Edinburgh, Aberdeen and Dundee. In fact, from their very beginning in the 1920s these clubs had been a cultural development rather than a fascist one and they further reinforced the Italian sense of identity.

Summary

- The Irish made up the biggest immigrant community in Scotland. The Catholic Irish stood out because of their religion and language. They faced persecution and discrimination and developed cultural and educational structures that emphasised their identity. However, they did integrate through the trade union and temperance movements.
- Protestant Irish made up about one in four of the Irish immigrants. With similarities in religion and background they generally integrated into the local Scottish communities easily.
- Irish Protestants brought the Orange Order to Scotland and provided the bulk of its membership. They were well represented in skilled trades in engineering and shipbuilding in particular.
- Jewish immigrants arrived in large numbers in the late nineteenth century. They formed a distinct community owing to their religion and language. They worked in jobs that were not a general threat to the native Scot, although they faced anti-semitism.
- Lithuanians arrived in Scotland fleeing persecution in Eastern Europe and worked in industries like coal mining. Initially they retained a distinct sense of identity, but by the 1920s many had left. Those that remained had largely integrated with their Scottish neighbours.
- Italian immigrants ran popular service industries that did not threaten Scottish jobs. The Italian community was accepted, but retained a sense of identity through patterns of origin, family and work.

Activities

You are going to create a character sketch for each of the five immigrant communities identified in the text above.

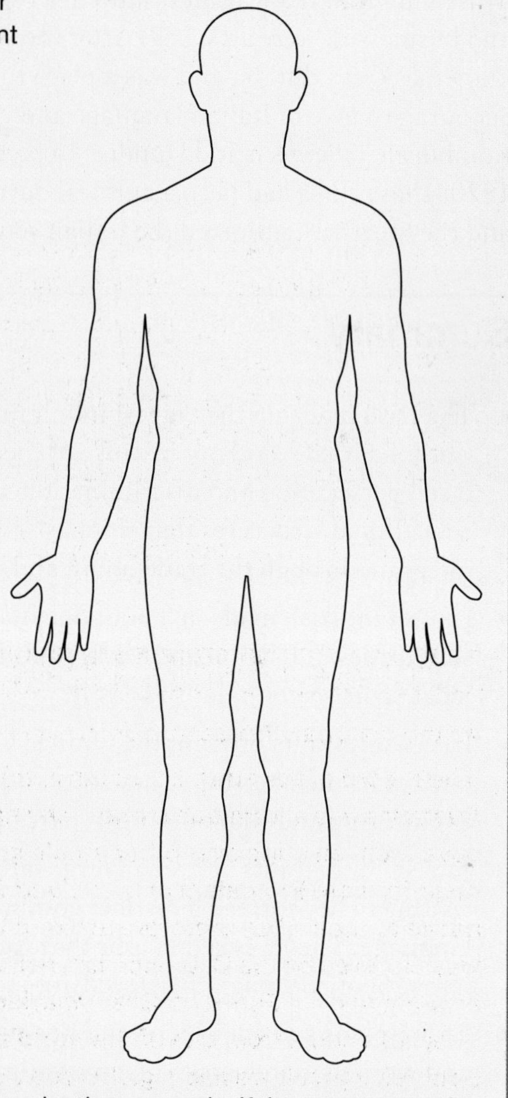

For each of the communities copy the image of a person into your notes. Position it in the centre of an A4 page and make sure it is large enough to fill the depth of the page.

Inside the figure write all those features which made this person different from the Scottish population. You might consider the following as a starting point:

- their religion
- their language.

Outside the figure write all the ways in which this person interacted with Scotland. You might consider the following as a starting point:

- jobs done
- areas of conflict
- areas of agreement.

When you have completed your five character sketches, cover up the heading for each of them and test your classmates on who the person is. If they can guess the nationality of the figure in the sketch then you must have done a good job!

4 The impact of Scots emigrants on the Empire

Scots settled abroad for a wide variety of reasons. Many travelled to places like Canada, Australia and New Zealand to start a new life. The attractions of cheap land and encouragement from governments and relatives persuaded them to go. However, depending on their motives and their subsequent success, between one quarter and one third of emigrants returned home to Scotland in the late nineteenth century. This was especially true of Scots who had emigrated to India. Scots abroad were uniquely placed to make a contribution to the development of the countries they settled in.

Source 4.1

As the historian Professor Tom Devine notes:

'The record of the emigrant Scots in the making of North America and Australasia is a formidable one. They had several advantages which gave them an edge over other ethnic groups. The overwhelming majority were Protestant and Lowland Scots, with English as their native tongue. They therefore avoided the religious discrimination that was suffered by the Catholic Irish, while maintaining a clear linguistic advantage over Germans, Scandinavians, French, Italians and others. They also came from one of the world's most advanced economies. Scottish agriculture had a global reputation for excellence and efficiency, while the nation had a leading position in areas such as banking, insurance, engineering, applied science, shipbuilding, coalmining and iron and steel manufacture.'

The impact of Scots on the Empire was very positive in many ways. This has to be balanced with more negative effects as the Scots were guilty of treating the native peoples of places like Australia and New Zealand very badly at times.

Canada

Source 4.2

Map of Canada

Canada was an attractive place for Scots to emigrate to, especially for Highlanders who were used to a farming life. It was also relatively easy to travel to Canada.

Source 4.3

Writer Jenni Calder comments:

'Crossing the Atlantic was not so daunting a prospect as voyaging half way around the world, and Scots generally knew a great deal more about Canada than about Australia or New Zealand.'

It's difficult to give exact figures but, in 1849, the *Scotsman* newspaper estimated that 20,000 Scots migrated to Canada between 1839 and 1849. Almost a hundred years later, half a million Scots migrated to Canada between 1900 and 1930.

Scots settled in areas like Ontario and Nova Scotia (Latin for 'New Scotland') and their influence can be seen in the numbers of people in Canada who claim Scottish ancestry today. Scots are considered to be the third largest ethnic group in Canada, and even the flags of parts of Canada show the influence of Scots.

Source 4.4

Flag of Nova Scotia

Economy and enterprise

Scots were very important to the Canadian economy, particularly in the development of trade in furs and timber, as well as in agriculture. They were also involved in banking and the development of the Canadian railway network.

Source 4.5

Author David S. MacMillan states:

'Recent studies in Canadian business and entrepreneurial history have shown clearly that Scots were very important and pre-eminent in trade, commerce and industry, and their influence as well as that of their descendants has largely moulded the economic outlook of Canada.'

Some industries, such as the paper industry, were wholly run by Scots. They were also heavily involved in the iron, steel, oil and gas industries. By the 1920s it has been calculated that one quarter of Canada's business leaders were born in Scotland, with another 25 per cent having Scottish-born fathers.

Source 4.6

This map shows the area around the Hudson Bay controlled by the Hudson Bay Company. It stretched for thousands of miles across what became known as Canada.

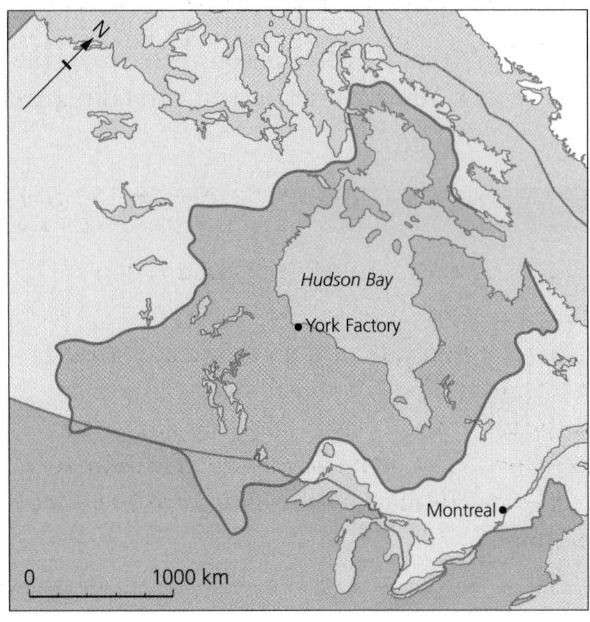

In the 1830s the most important trade that Scots were involved in was the fur trade. The fur trade in Canada is associated with the Hudson's Bay Company and it was dominated by Scots, in particular George Simpson. Historian Michael Fry described Simpson as being like an 'Emperor of the Plains to his awestruck underlings' (*The Scottish Empire*, p. 107).

The Hudson's Bay Company recruited heavily in the Western and Northern Isles of Scotland. Orkney was a favourite place to find willing workers. Such recruits frequently worked for the company to pay off debts built up in Scotland, before returning home.

Source 4.7

George Simpson, born in Dingwall, Ross-shire, in 1792, worked for the Hudson's Bay Company, becoming Governor-in-Chief of company territory in Canada from 1821 until his death in Montreal in 1860.

However, the fur trade never employed vast numbers of emigrants. It was farming and industry that attracted most new emigrants. Scots had settled in the fertile districts of Ontario for years before 1830, but the Clearances encouraged a large number of Highlanders to move there. In eastern Ontario, by 1849 one in six inhabitants of the 17,500 people living there had the surname MacDonnell or MacDonald. Astonishingly this part of Canada made up the largest Gaelic-speaking population outside Scotland at that time.

Scots quickly gained a reputation for being hard working, risk-taking and seeking to improve their life.

Source 4.8

Dr Thomas Rolph from Upper Canada wrote this about one of his employees:

'I will give you proof of one from Aberdeen whom I hired at $16.00 a month as a farm labourer. I had an Englishman at the same time to whom I paid the same wages. I was astonished that the Scotsman never came to me for his wages; he said he wanted to save them for a certain purpose; at the end of three years he took nearly $100 off me and purchased land of his own.'

Scots also had a good reputation because they brought to Canada new ideas on how to farm. One such development was the introduction of crop rotation, which helped to improve greatly the amount of crops produced.

Adam Fergusson journeyed through Canada in the 1830s and describes how a fellow Scot, from Angus, had made a successful life there.

Source 4.9

Adam Fergusson:

'He is an example of what an industrious and steady man may do for himself in Canada. He came out in 1817. He soon found employment and in time took a lease of a farm which he finds to succeed extremely well. His wheat and potatoes he says are excellent. He uses horses in preference to oxen: has iron ploughs, and follows what he called a sort of rotation that produces crop yields better than ever before.'

The development of Canadian industry

Scots made a significant impact on the development of Canadian industry.

Source 4.10

J.A. McIntyre describes the impact on Montreal:

'As industry began to develop in Montreal, particularly in engineering, Scots from the Clydeside shipyards, from the engine building works in Motherwell and various engineering firms in the Glasgow area, began to emigrate to Canada. Even in the first decade of the twentieth century either first or second generation Scottish immigrants still dominated the industries.'

Railways

One example of an industrial development that illustrates the huge influence of Scots in the Canadian economy is the Transatlantic Canadian Pacific Railway. Strong support for the railway came from Sir John A. MacDonald, the first Prime Minister of Canada. MacDonald was a Scot who was born in Glasgow in 1815. His family emigrated to Ontario in 1820. MacDonald was a very successful Canadian Prime Minister, serving for a total of eighteen years.

MacDonald believed that building a railway across all of Canada would unite the vast territories of the country. The railway would also open up the interior of this vast country for further economic exploitation. British Columbia on the Pacific coast had made the development of such a transport link a condition of joining the Canadian confederation.

Source 4.11

Canadian election poster, 1891, featuring Scottish-born Sir John A. MacDonald, the first Prime Minister of Canada.

There were also political reasons for developing the railway network. MacDonald was a strong supporter of links with Britain and saw the railway as a way of ensuring independence from the United States of America. The election poster in Source 4.11 unites these themes of loyalty to Britain and economic development of Canada.

Scots were also important in the financing and engineering of the railway. George Stephen at the Bank of Montreal and John Rose in London helped finance it, while another Scot, Sandford Fleming, was the railway's main engineer.

Source 4.12

Advert explaining the attractions of Canada through the Canadian Pacific Railway.

The Transatlantic Canadian Pacific Railway was completed in 1885. It was an impressive piece of engineering, but much of its length passed through undeveloped and poorly populated land. The railway was important in attracting immigrants to Canada to settle land around the railway. The company offered cheap land and an attractive travel package for immigrants. In doing so it was creating a market and long-term wealth for the company! Many Scots were amongst those attracted by such an offer.

Source 4.13

Writer Pierre Berton explains the dominance of the Scots in Canada:

'For the Scots it was work, save and study; study, save and work. Though they formed only one fifteenth of the population, Scots controlled the fur trade, the great banking and financial houses, the major educational institutions and, to a considerable degree, the government. The Canadian Pacific Railway was built to a large extent by Irish navvies and Irish contractors; but it was the Scots who held the top jobs.'

Education, culture and religion

Scots were important in the development of the Canadian education system. At first the lead was taken by the Church. In 1831 Bishop MacEachern formed a college, and this foundation was the beginning of higher education in Prince Edward Island.

Presbyterian [Protestant] Scots were also involved. Thomas McCulloch, a Presbyterian Scot, was the first principal of Pictou Academy in Nova Scotia, for example. Its curriculum was based on that offered at Glasgow University. Although it started as a college to train ministers for the Church, by 1831 it had also opened a grammar school. By 1842 the college was closed, but the school grew and still survives today.

Other examples include the world-famous McGill University, which was founded in 1821 with money from the estate of James McGill, a merchant and politician who had emigrated from Glasgow. Queen's University in Kingston, Canada, was founded in 1841 by the Church of Scotland. Its first principal was a Scot, the Reverend Dr Thomas Liddell. The University of Toronto was also founded by a Scot called James Strachan.

Scottish influence can also be seen in the development of the curriculum in Canadian universities. Scottish universities had a broad curriculum that was interested in practical subjects. This belief travelled with the emigrants. When William Brydone Jack, a Scottish graduate from St Andrews University, arrived as principal of King's College in Fredericton, Canada, he introduced more practical subjects for study. King's College became the first Canadian university to offer a degree in Engineering in 1854.

Source 4.14

Writer D.C. Masters states:

'The long-run influence of the Scots in Canadian higher education has been profound. In the Roman Catholic world Scots helped to organise colleges which preserved the Scottish identity. In the Protestant world in Canada its intellectual discipline produced men with a capacity for sheer hard work and with a penetrating, critical spirit.'

Scotland also had a huge impact on the broader culture of Canada. Canadian literature has been influenced by Scottish writers from Robert Burns to Robert Louis Stevenson and Sir Walter Scott.

Source 4.15

Author Elizabeth Waterson believes that the Scots influence is down to the similarities that Canada has with Scotland:

'In Canada, as in Scotland, two languages, two religions, and two cultures have existed.'

The Scots' influence on Canadian culture also had a lot to do with the Scottish-dominated educational system and publishing houses. Scottish Gaelic culture can be seen in the way in which Canada embraced the ceilidh, bagpipes, tartan, the fiddle and even curling!

Source 4.16

George Emmerson highlights the fact that the Canadian army shared in the Scottish identity:

'If Highland games and dancing, Gaelic mods, bagpiping, fiddling and, to some extent, curling, cannot testify to the strength of Gaelic cultural influence in Canada, one cannot ignore the many war memorials surmounted by kilted soldiers.'

Source 4.17

Curling on the St Lawrence, Montreal, Quebec

Native societies

Canada was a harsh environment. When emigrants arrived, they met native people who had lived and survived there for many years. At first, the Scottish, English and French fur traders traded with the Native Indian tribes that lived in Canada. Indeed, the Hudson's Bay Company could not have carried on their fur trade without them. To begin with the Native Indian tribes hunted for animal skins and traded this for European goods made from metal and cloth. Commercial and personal relationships also developed between the Scots and the 'First Peoples' as the local native population was called. For example, company doctors tended the Indian sick, and European traders also intermarried with the Indian tribes. The results of this union between European and Indian are called Métis people. The Métis people were skilled hunters, and could also speak to both the native peoples and the incoming settlers. As such they were extremely valuable people in the development of the fur trade.

As the fur traders were followed by settlers so the role of the Native Indians became even more important.

Source 4.18

Writer Jenni Calder points out:

'Without [the Native Indians'] support, many settlers would not have got through their first winter, and many of the Company's employees would never have learnt to adapt to so harsh an environment. Without the Native skills of making canoes of cedar ribs and birch bark and snowshoes of birch and sinew, of recognising the sounds and movements of animals, of reading changes in weather, many Scottish communities would not have lasted.'

However, the traditional life of the Native Indians was changed forever by contact with immigrants like the Scots. Not all immigrants were respectful of the skills and culture of the Native Indians. Some immigrants saw them as 'savages' who were not 'civilised'. The immigrant Scots who had been displaced from their land in the Highlands by the Clearances were perfectly capable of doing exactly the same thing to the Native Indians in Canada.

As the numbers of settlers increased, the Native Indians were increasingly pushed off their land. Eventually the Métis people fought back in the North-West rebellion of 1885 but the Métis leader, Louis Reil, was executed. The march of the Canadian Government across land once controlled by the Hudson's Bay Company continued and brought with it big changes to the way of life of the native people.

Australia

Although further away than Canada, Australia was also a popular destination for Scottish emigrants. Again, it offered opportunities for the enterprising Scot, although the first Scots to arrive there were convicts! Scots made an impact in many areas of Australian life (see Source 4.19).

Source 4.19

Writer Arthur Herman comments:

'By the 1880s Australia had the fastest growing economy and the highest per capita income in the world. Scots were active in every major aspect of Australian life, including business, education, religion and farming.'

Source 4.20

Map of Australia

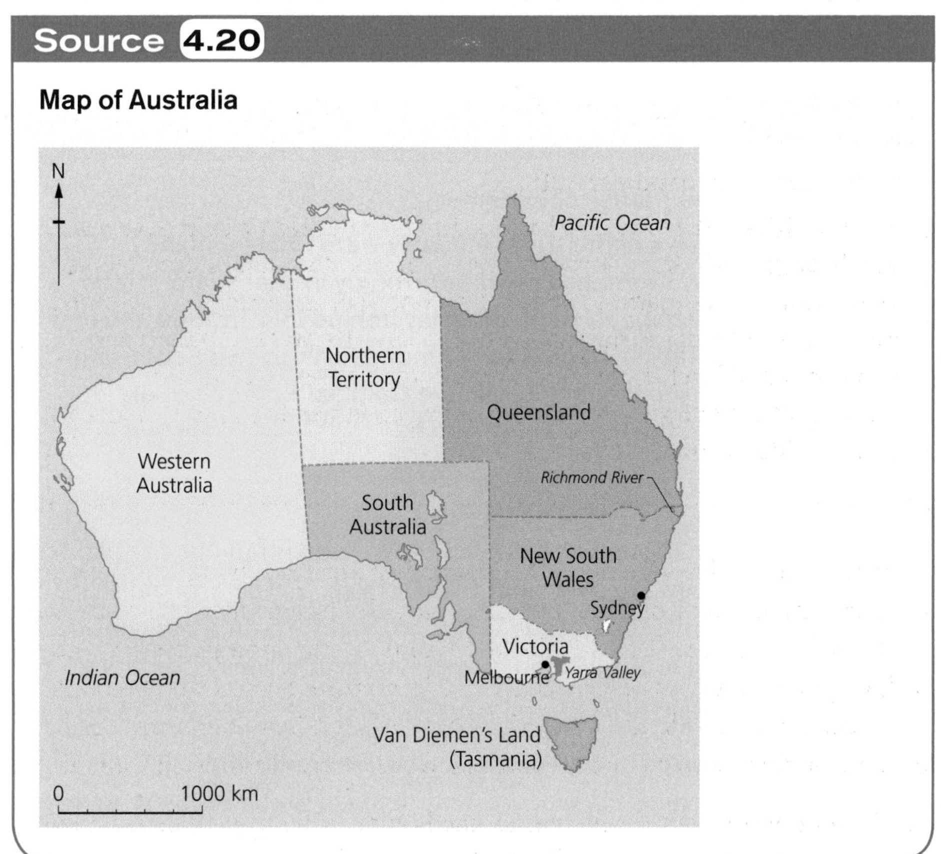

Economy and enterprise

Scots were important in the development of farming in Australia. They had the necessary skills to develop sheep farming, in particular. George Russell, originally from Fife, was managing 8000 head of sheep and almost 300 cattle in Van Diemen's Land (modern-day Tasmania), Australia, in 1839. He earned an annual salary of £100 and a share of the profits each year. By the time of his death in 1888, he left over £318,000, a huge sum of money. It was a Scot, John Macarthur, who introduced the merino sheep to Australia.

Scotland was also a significant investor in developing agriculture in Australia. For example, Scottish investment was used to set up huge sheep runs in New South Wales and Victoria. One example was the Clyde Company, which was formed in 1836 to support and manage sheep farming businesses in Tasmania, although it moved its business to the more profitable Victoria by 1839. Three wealthy Scots formed Neil Back and Company, which developed 44,000 acres of land.

Scots also made a more specialised contribution to the sugar and wine industries in Australia (Source 4.21).

Source 4.21

Professor Malcolm Prentis comments:

'Most of the pioneers of the sugar industry were Scots and they continued their involvement almost as strongly in later years. A little-noted Scottish-Caribbean connection lay behind this. In 1869, the first sugar mill was established on the Richmond River by two Scots, and another Scot was the first to interest the Colonial Sugar Refinery Company (CSR) in the Richmond's sugar.'

In the wine industry, the name of Samuel McWilliam is famous. He planted his first vines at Corowa in New South Wales in 1877. The firm did well and the McWilliam family subsequently developed vineyards in six regions in three states. Scots were also behind the development of vineyards in Victoria in the Yarra Valley as well as in South Australia and Western Australia.

Scots were also involved in developing Australian trade, mining, manufacturing, shipping, engineering and finance. In the 1830s Scots were heavily involved in the development of the whaling industry: for example, Alexander Imlay from Aberdeen operating from Tasmania. The Scots' involvement in mining can be seen from the 1840s in New South Wales and the coal mining developments around Newcastle. James and Alexander Brown built up a large concern there and employed many fellow Scots in the mine. In the 1860s the mine was managed by another Scot, James Fletcher.

As late as the 1920s and 1930s Scots were coming from Lanarkshire and Ayrshire to work in the New South Wales mines. Yet another Scot, Robert McCracken from Ayrshire, developed brewing in Melbourne.

Robert Campbell from Greenock played such an important role in developing Australian trade that he was known as 'The father of Australian Commerce'. When he died in 1846 it could be said that his all-round impact on many aspects of Australian life summed up the impact of the Scots in one man! Campbell is an excellent example of an enterprising Scot who had wide interests and took risks in making his riches. At the age of 27 he moved to Calcutta in India to be with his brother and developed business interests there before moving to Sydney, Australia. There he was a general merchant before developing Australia's first shipyard as well as a sheep farm! A wealthy man, he gave money to religious and educational establishments, and also participated in New South Wales politics before his retirement.

Source 4.22

Melbourne Iron works, founded by John Buncle (1822–89) from Edinburgh. Buncle was a locomotive builder and is a fine example of a skilled engineer who transferred his skills to benefit countries abroad. He arrived in Melbourne in 1852 when gold fever was at its height. He set up on his own and found work supplying farming tools. Like many other successful Scots he entered local politics as a councillor and was mayor of Hotham, Melbourne, twice. He also took an interest in education, helping found the Hotham School of Design.

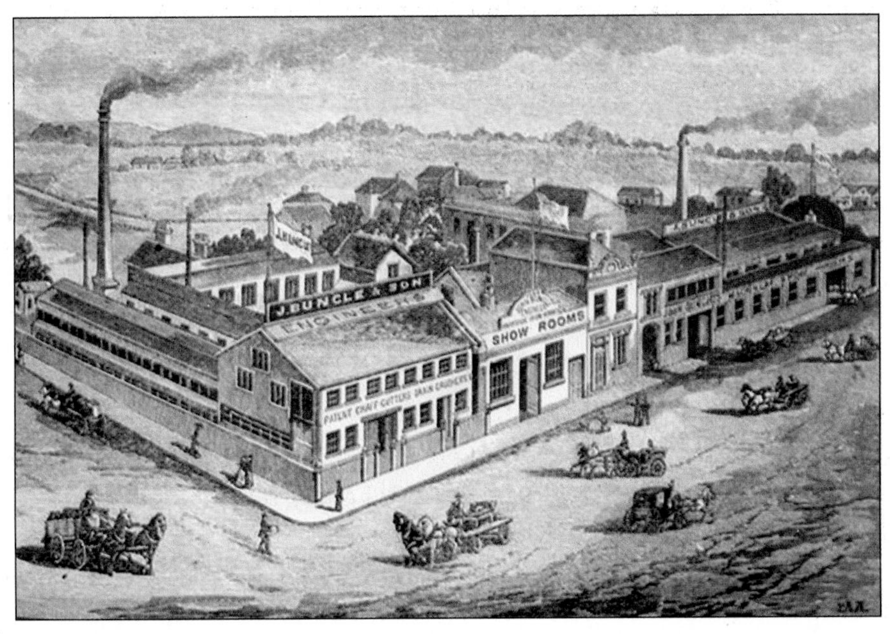

Even the finance behind many Australian businesses was Scottish, with Scots influencing the development of the Australian banking system.

Source 4.23

Malcolm Prentis writes:

'The Australian banking system was created out of a blend of English and Scottish traditions – it started mainly English but rapidly came to resemble the Scottish pattern: for example, central banks with branches and interest-bearing deposits. The first bank, the Bank of New South Wales, was founded in 1817 with the encouragement of the Scottish governor, Macquarie. The first chief executive was Ulster-Scot, J.T. Campbell, and more than a quarter of his successors to 1900 were Scots.'

Scots dominated many shipping firms in Australia, as well as providing the shipping itself! One of the most famous was the company of McIlwraith McEacharn. Andrew McIlwraith and Malcolm McEacharn set the business up in London in 1875. McEacharn eventually moved to Australia and set up the first successful transportation of refrigerated meat to Britain. The company also had a very successful trade in carrying emigrants to Australia as well as other cargo.

Source 4.24

McEacharn & Company's SS *Cloncurry*

Source 4.25

Malcolm McEacharn became Mayor of Melbourne in 1897 and held the post for three years. He was elected as a member of the Australian Parliament in 1901.

Education, culture and religion

Source 4.26

Writer Malcolm Prentis states:

'The Presbyterian Church was the most important Scottish institution brought to Australia.'

The Church was a familiar presence and a place of worship for Scottish immigrants. Its other importance lies in shaping the people of Australia and their culture through education.

Most Scottish immigrants were Presbyterian and their Church (or Kirk, as it was known) supported the development of education. These schools were based on the model of parish schools that had been developed in Scotland. There were 42 parish schools in New South Wales by 1850. As the Government in Australia began to take an interest in developing a system of education, many of these parish schools became part of the state education system by the 1870s.

In the state of Queensland, Scots led the education system. The head of Queensland's teacher training, and head of its most important school, between 1874 and 1906 was James Semple Kerr. Kerr was born in Stewarton, Ayrshire. He was a Presbyterian and was famous for his hard work and discipline with both teachers and pupils! Presbyterian Scots also set up 'high schools' for secondary education. These schools offered a wide curriculum for the pupils and emphasised the need to do good work in society.

In Victoria there were a large number of Presbyterian secondary schools, and Melbourne Academy even became known as the Scotch College. Alexander Morrison, who was its second headmaster between 1857 and 1903, changed the school's curriculum to be more in line with his old school: Elgin Academy in Morayshire, Scotland. He added subjects like science and modern languages to the curriculum.

Schools that were set up and run by Scots like this were important as they produced many of the political, economic, military and educational leaders of the future.

Although less 'Scottish' than Scottish Canadians, in terms of their use of Scottish imagery like tartan, Scottish Australians have been important contributors to Australian identity. Two of Australia's national songs, 'Waltzing Mathilda' and 'Advance Australia Fair', were written by Scots in the late nineteenth century. Scots' involvement in the poetry of Australia can be seen in a collection of poetry produced in 1909. Over 25 per cent of the poets were born in Scotland or had Scottish parents.

Native societies

Because of their expansion of farming land Scottish emigrants came into increasing contact with the native Aboriginal people of Australia. There are a large number of examples of ill-treatment of the native peoples by Scots (as well as by many other emigrant peoples). The 'Hornet Bank' massacre of 1857 shows how conflict arose as farming land began to eat into traditional Aboriginal land. In 1854 the Fraser family leased land in Queensland to run a large ranch (or 'station', as it was called in Australia) for sheep and cattle farming at Hornet Bank. The local Aboriginal people found their traditional way of life was severely disrupted by such farming. They were also often treated cruelly by the white population. They attacked the Fraser family homestead in 1857, killing eight of the Fraser family and three other white Europeans. William Fraser, a member of the family who had been away at the time of the massacre, killed at least 100 Aboriginal people in retaliation.

Source 4.27

This artwork from around 1860 shows dissident aborigines being suppressed by native troopers.

NATIVE TROOPERS DISPERSING A "MYALL" CAMP.

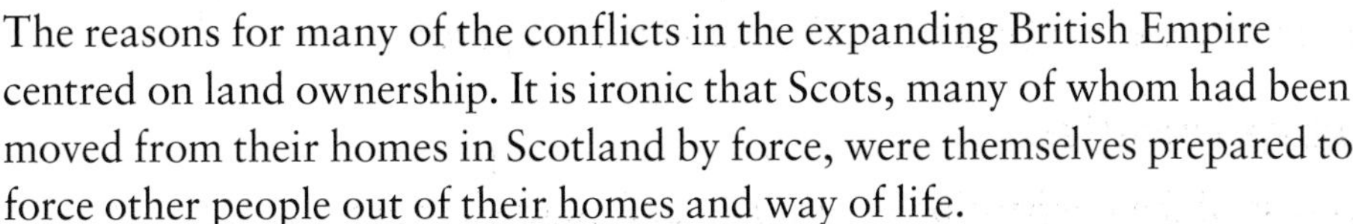

The reasons for many of the conflicts in the expanding British Empire centred on land ownership. It is ironic that Scots, many of whom had been moved from their homes in Scotland by force, were themselves prepared to force other people out of their homes and way of life.

However, there is also a lot of evidence of Scots who actively sought good relations with the local population. Men such as Francis Armstrong learned the language and culture of the local Aboriginal people he met. Others like John and Alec Mortimer in Queensland were active supporters of Aboriginal rights. Some Scottish immigrants married Aboriginal women. In New South Wales surnames like Cameron and Campbell exist in the Aborigine communities.

One interesting Aboriginal–Scot was Douglas Grant, who was born in the 1880s and was adopted by a Scot. He went to the Scot's College in Sydney and even played in the pipe band. He fought in the Australia Imperial Force during the First World War and was captured by the Germans in 1917. One story about him tells of when he visited his adoptive father's village in Scotland after the war. He spoke to a local Scottish shop girl who is supposed to have said, 'There's a Scotty here frae Australia, but he's been burnt black by the sun'.

Source 4.28

Aboriginal–Scot Private Douglas Grant (far left), with two British soldiers

New Zealand

Source 4.29

Map of New Zealand

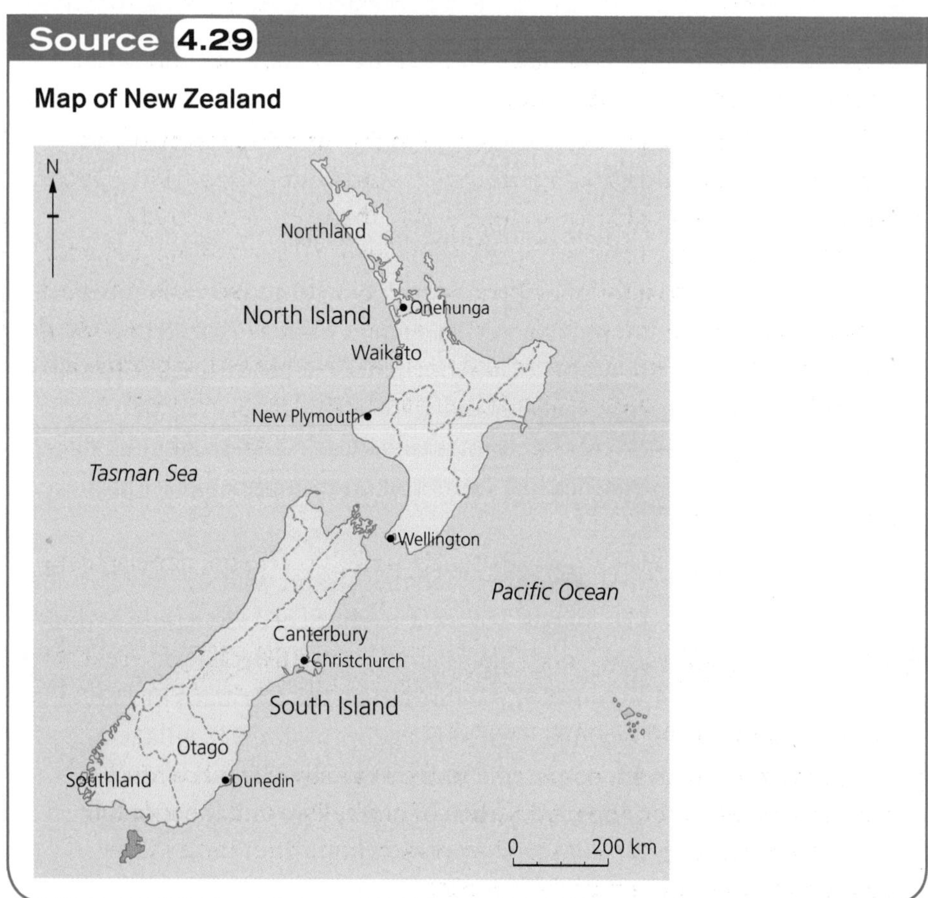

Scots were very important in the development of New Zealand. By 1891 approximately 25 per cent of the UK-born population in New Zealand was Scottish. In terms of the numbers of emigrants, one in five were Scots; by the 1920s it was as high as one in three. This has led to a significant Scottish influence in New Zealand.

Source 4.30

Authors Jock Philips and Terry Hearn state:

'New Zealand was well over twice as Scottish as the homeland.'

Parts of New Zealand were influenced by Scottish immigrants because of the numbers of Scots who chose to settle there. Some parts of New Zealand became more Scottish than others as a result. Presbyterian Scottish settlers created the town of Dunedin, which became an important settlement in New Zealand. Scots were also behind the founding of Otago in the South Island and were important in Southland. As with other parts of the Empire, Scots were considered to be good immigrants because they were Protestant, hard-working and well-educated.

Source 4.31

Historian Michael Fry in his book *The Scottish Empire* describes the Scots' success in New Zealand:

'The price of land fell at a time when, with the introduction of sheep, the revenue from it was rising. Nothing could better suit a thrifty Scots faming community, which now testified to the value of carefully selecting colonists. Their prosperity allowed fulfilment of the plans for ample provision in religion and education. Churches, schools, libraries abounded, while Dunedin had a university by 1869. Otago even looked Scottish. The settlers left it treeless, unlike the neighbouring province of Canterbury, occupied by the English and extensively afforested.'

Economy and enterprise

Lowland Scots were important to New Zealand's economic development (Source 4.32).

Source 4.32

Jock Philips and Terry Hearn comment:

'Since so many of them grew up in or close to big cities, Lowland migrants understood the institutions of capitalism and the value of investment for long-term gain. They played important roles in the economic development of the country.'

Examples of Scots' success in New Zealand

John Ross from Halkirk in the Highlands and Robert Glendinning from Fife set up a wholesale drapery business in Dunedin in the 1860s. At this time gold had been discovered and the business did well as Dunedin was at the centre of the economic development of New Zealand. The business developed into clothing manufacturing. Ross and Glendinning bought sheep farms and developed clothing factories; they became rich men, dominating the textile industry. Ross used some of his wealth to help the Presbyterian Church set up a training college for its ministers in New Zealand.

Other Scots were also successful:

- Scots founded New Zealand's paper-making industry and were important engineers and shipbuilders.
- Peter and David Duncan, originally from Forfar, developed a successful business in Agricultural implements in Christchurch.
- Henry Niccol was born in Greenock in 1819. In 1843 he set up a shipyard in Auckland. Between 1843 and 1887 over 180 ships were built in the company yard.
- Many Scots were skilled farmers and influenced the development of New Zealand through sheep and mixed farming. Donald Reid, from Perthshire, arrived in New Zealand in 1849. He became a farm labourer, but purchased his first land in 1852. By the time of his death in 1919 he had built up an estate of 6300 acres and was a rich man.

Source 4.33

Dunedin, on New Zealand's South Island, was established by Scottish settlers.

Source 4.34

The Northern Steam Ship Company was founded by Alexander McGregor, who was born in Nova Scotia but was of Scottish descent. The Scottish influence can be seen in the timetable; the company flag includes the St Andrew's cross.

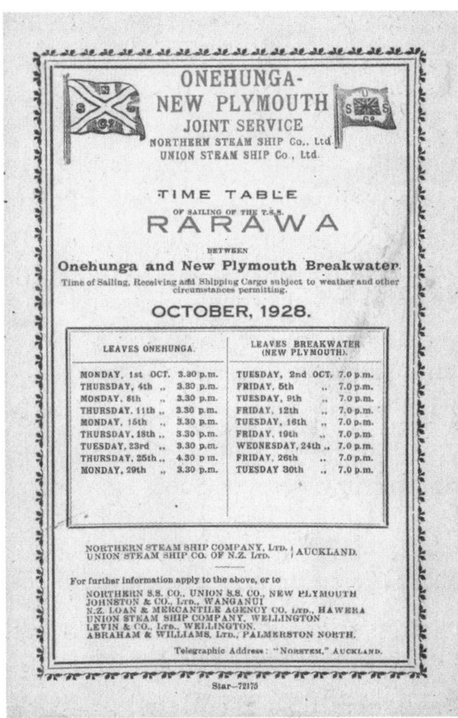

ONEHUNGA-
NEW PLYMOUTH
JOINT SERVICE
NORTHERN STEAM SHIP Co., Ltd
UNION STEAM SHIP Co., Ltd.

TIME TABLE
OF SAILING OF THE T.S.S.
RARAWA
BETWEEN
Onehunga and New Plymouth Breakwater.
Time of Sailing, Receiving and Shipping Cargo subject to weather and other circumstances permitting.

OCTOBER, 1928.

LEAVES ONEHUNGA.		LEAVES BREAKWATER (NEW PLYMOUTH).	
MONDAY, 1st OCT.	3.30 p.m.	TUESDAY, 2nd OCT.	7.0 p.m.
THURSDAY, 4th „	3.30 p.m.	FRIDAY, 5th „	7.0 p.m.
MONDAY, 8th „	3.30 p.m.	TUESDAY, 9th „	7.0 p.m.
THURSDAY, 11th „	3.30 p.m.	FRIDAY, 12th „	7.0 p.m.
MONDAY, 15th „	3.30 p.m.	TUESDAY, 16th „	7.0 p.m.
THURSDAY, 18th „	3.30 p.m.	FRIDAY, 19th „	7.0 p.m.
TUESDAY, 23rd „	3.30 p.m.	WEDNESDAY, 24th „	7.0 p.m.
THURSDAY, 25th „	4.30 p.m.	FRIDAY, 26th „	7.0 p.m.
MONDAY, 29th „	3.30 p.m.	TUESDAY 30th „	7.0 p.m.

NORTHERN STEAM SHIP COMPANY, LTD. } AUCKLAND.
UNION STEAM SHIP CO. OF N.Z. LTD. }

For further information apply to the above, or to
NORTHERN S.S. CO., UNION S.S. CO., NEW PLYMOUTH
JOHNSTON & CO., LTD., WANGANUI
N.Z. LOAN & MERCANTILE AGENCY CO. LTD., HAWERA
UNION STEAM SHIP COMPANY, WELLINGTON
LEVIN & CO., LTD., WELLINGTON.
ABRAHAM & WILLIAMS, LTD., PALMERSTON NORTH.

Telegraphic Address: "NORSTEM," AUCKLAND.

Star—72175

Education, culture and religion

In terms of a long-lasting impact on culture, education was an important area that was influenced by the Scots. In 1872 the Scottish Education Act was passed. This made education compulsory for all children in Scotland between the ages of 5 and 13, and it was provided free. This system became the basis for New Zealand's education system, introduced in 1877.

Otago, with its Scottish influence, was important in terms of education developments. A Scot called Learmonth Dalrymple was behind New Zealand's first school for girls, which opened in Otago in 1871. The first principal of the school was Margaret Gordon Burn, a fellow Scot. New Zealand's first university was opened in 1869 in Otago, and the Scottish university with its broad curriculum provided the basis for it.

Scottish influence can also be seen in the way in which medicine was seen as being important. In 1875 the first medical school in New Zealand opened up in Otago. The first head of medicine was a Scot called John Scott, and the professor of physiology, John Malcolm, was a fellow countryman.

Scottish immigrants had an important role in the development of New Zealand's holidays. Owing to their Protestant traditions for many years Scots did not celebrate Christmas; instead New Year was the important holiday, although this was not a holiday in England. New Zealand recognised New Year's Day as a holiday by the late nineteenth century. Events were held on this day to celebrate Scottish culture, such as the Caledonian Games. Scottish foods like porridge and scones have also become important parts of the New Zealand diet.

Native societies

Scots, like other immigrants, had a big impact on the Maori people of New Zealand. The Maori people are the descendants of Polynesian settlers from South-East Asia. In the 1830s the population of Maori living in New Zealand was over 100,000 but there were only about 2000 European settlers (known as Pakeha) in New Zealand.

To begin with, the Scots had a positive relationship with the Maori in the Otago/Southland area. There is some evidence that the Maori helped early Scottish colonists survive the harsh winters of 1848 and 1849 by supplying them with potatoes and pork. However, Scots were also involved in taking land from the Maori.

By the 1830s the British Government had become concerned about the behaviour of some of the settlers towards the Maori. The Maori sought British Government protection and in 1840 the Treaty of Waitangi was signed.

Source 4.35

Maori Chiefs recognise British sovereignty by signing the treaty of Waitangi.

The Treaty of Waitangi gave the British the right to rule New Zealand. In return the British promised to protect the rights of Maori people and their land. The main problem with the Treaty was that the two peoples had very different ideas of what it meant to own land. The Maori sold land to the colonists through the control of British Government representatives.

Problems arose as demand for land increased when more and more colonists arrived. Sometimes it proved difficult to work out who owned the Maori land. As a result, sometimes the wrong people gained money from the land deals and settlers moved onto land which had not necessarily been sold.

The impact of Scottish settlers on Maori life therefore was often bad. As well as being involved in land deals that took land from the Maori, many Scots wanted to farm and this led to the clearance of trees from land, which had an impact on the traditional life of the Maori.

The Maori people became unhappy and in 1872 conflict broke out.

This led to lasting bitterness on the part of the Maori. Tom Brooking from Otago University in New Zealand has commented that the Maori have been forgotten and have become virtually invisible on the margins of Otago life. However, some Scots were very sympathetic to the situation the Maori found themselves in.

Source 4.36

Historian Michael Fry comments:

'Donald Maclean, an emigrant from Tiree to New Zealand ... learned the Maoris' language... In his new home he made a political career, and rose to be Native Minister in 1877–80. He was the first to take the job seriously, trying to ensure that white colonists always regularly purchased their land from the chiefs, and that these sold it of their own free will. The Maoris would thus ... choose how much of their country to keep as reserves for themselves, while acquiring the capital to develop their own agriculture.'

Similar sympathies can be seen with Arthur Charles Hamilton Gordon, First Baron Stanmore, who was appointed as Governor of New Zealand between 1880 and 1882. He sided with the Maori in land disputes, which brought him into conflict with his own government in New Zealand.

There is evidence of intermarriage between Scots and Maori, with more than one instance of a Maori with the Scottish surname of Stewart!

Source 4.37

Arthur Charles Hamilton Gordon, Governor of New Zealand between 1880 and 1882.

Source 4.38

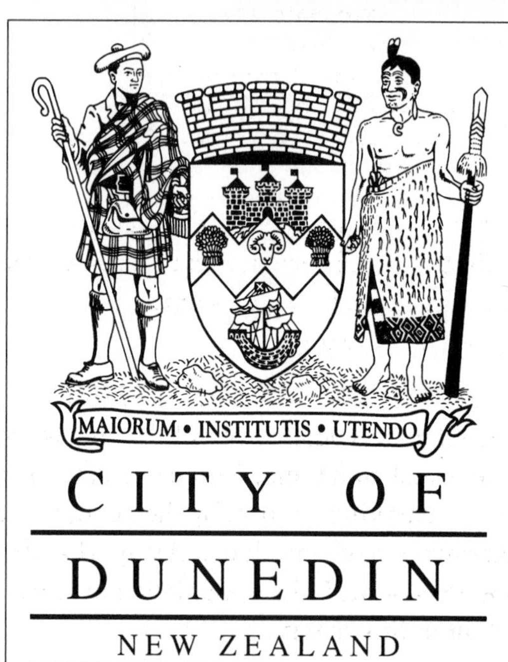

The interaction between Scot and Maori is clear in the Coat of Arms for Dunedin in New Zealand!

India

Source 4.39

Map of India around 1830

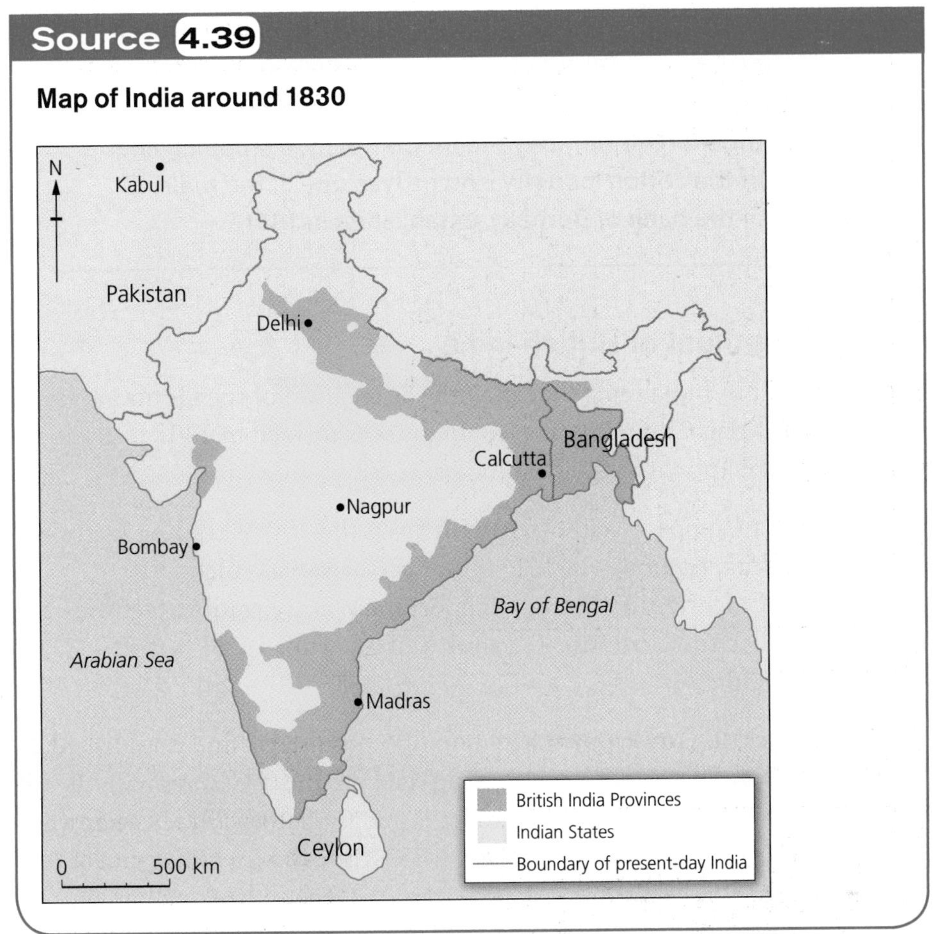

In 1830 India included the area of land that is modern India, Pakistan, Bangladesh and Sri Lanka. By 1830 Scots had been in India for some time. Scots had an impact on how India was ruled, how it developed economically and how its society was to develop.

Before 1830 Scots had been of great importance in extending British influence into India. They were merchants, soldiers and politicians. By 1830 times were changing regarding the British and India. Before this date their interest had been to do with trade and making a profit. By the middle of the nineteenth century they were determined to change India in ways that they felt would improve India. The opinions of the Indian population did not always matter. Scots were important in this change.

Scots had become involved in trading with India through the East India Company, but also as independent traders. The East India Company had a hold on trade for many years and, after this ended, the Scots' involvement in the economic development of India increased.

Source 4.40

Writer Alex Cain comments:

In 1836 after the ending of the Company's monopolies, the Bombay Chamber of Commerce was founded by one of Bombay's many Scottish traders, John Skinner, of the firm of that name. Skinner was a leading member of the Bombay Steam Company, a shipping line important for the cotton industry, and he was one of the main promoters of the bank of Bombay, established in 1841.'

The development of British India

British interest in India really began with the creation of the Honourable East India Trading Company. The company was formed in 1708 to trade with what were known as the East Indies.

The East India Company had three main bases (known as trading factories) in India: Madras, Bombay and Calcutta. Each area was ruled by a governor. As Calcutta was the most important of these trading factories, its leader was called the Governor-General, and was ruler of all British settlement in India.

In 1784 the British Government began to take an interest and established a 'Board of Control' in London, overseeing the East India Company. This system of two British authorities in India lasted until 1858. After what was known in Britain as the Indian Mutiny in 1857, the British Government assumed direct control of India. The Governor-General became known as the Viceroy. When Queen Victoria accepted the title of 'Empress of India' in 1887 the 'Indian Empire' or 'Raj' was born. Scots were involved in all areas of its development.

Perhaps the most controversial Scot to serve in India was James Andrew Broun-Ramsay, 1st Marquess of Dalhousie. Dalhousie was made Governor-General of India in 1848. He served until 1856. During his time as governor he developed a plan to build railway lines to connect the main regions of India as well as a telegraph communication system. He also encouraged a national postal service and the development of schools, roads and irrigation. Such developments both modernised and unified India. However, Dalhousie also actively pursued the policy of 'lapse and annexation', where if the ruling Indian king of a province/state did not have a natural heir the British took over their land.

Source 4.41

Dalhousie in 1850. He was one of a number of Scots who were to serve as Governors, then Viceroys, of India before it gained independence from Britain in 1947.

In the lands taken over by the British, Dalhousie banned the practices of *suttee* and *thuggee*. *Suttee* was the Hindu practice where a widow would voluntarily throw herself (or be forced to do so) on the funeral pyre of her husband. According to legend a British military officer who had conquered the Indian province of Sind was approached by a delegation of Hindu leaders complaining about his trying to end *suttee*. He is supposed to have said: 'You say that it is your custom to burn widows. Very well. We also have a custom: when men burn a woman alive, we tie a rope around their necks and we hang them. Build your funeral pyre; [then] beside it, my carpenters will build a gallows. You may follow your custom. And then we will follow ours.'

Thuggee was a term used for an organised cult of killers in India. They specialised in killing travellers quickly by strangulation using a thick, strong cord or cloth. The British stopped this practice. They hung over 500 Thugs between 1830 and 1841. This is where the British word 'thug' comes from!

Dalhousie was a far-sighted man in terms of many of the developments he started in India. However, he is also a good example of someone with what we might call a superior attitude. Like many at this time he firmly believed that the British were superior to the Indians and that people like himself were there to 'improve' the lives of the Indians through rational and efficient administration similar to that of the West (see Source 4.42).

Source 4.42

Historian Michael Fry sums up the 'superior' attitudes of many British and Scots:

'[Indians were] labouring under the burdens of superstition, tyranny, privilege and caste, which kept their religion, government, law and learning in a primitive state. The future lay in Westernisation.'

Westernisation meant many things, ranging from opening up India for trade to imposing good administration and ending 'savage' practices. Under such thinking, it seemed perfectly logical for the British to take over the corrupt province of Oudh. However, such moves were very unpopular in India at the time and led to the growth of anti-British feeling, eventually resulting in mutiny.

On the other hand, some commentators see the Scottish influence in India in a positive way (see Source 4.43). Charles James Napier was the Scottish soldier who conquered the Indian province of Sindh (in modern day Pakistan) in 1842. He is credited with creating a police force to keep order as well as develop the province economically.

Source 4.43

Historian Arthur Herman paints a rosy picture of the Scots and improvement:

'For native peoples, the British might not be their first choice. But, in many cases, thanks to Scots like Napier, they were better than what they had.'

The Indian Mutiny

The Indian Mutiny broke out in 1857. For many Indians today, the Indian Mutiny is called the First Indian War of Independence. What is not in doubt is that Indian troops (or *sepoys*) serving in the East India Company army rebelled. The causes are many, but dislike of British influence and rule, as well as fear of conversion to Christianity, were important factors. The rebellion was mainly in the north and centre of India and was only crushed in 1858. It threatened the power of the East India Company and was the reason why the British Government took direct control of India in its aftermath.

Scottish soldiers were very important in the British crushing of the rebellion. Most of the senior commanders were Scottish: Generals Colin Campbell, James Hope Grant, James Outram and Hugh Rose.

Source 4.44

Sir Colin Campbell, Lord Clyde (1792–1863). Engraving from 1858. Campbell is widely credited with the quick suppression of the Indian Mutiny. Careful planning and hard fighting, using Scottish, other British and loyal Indian troops led to success.

In July 1857, during the Indian Mutiny, the British inhabitants of the garrison town of Cawnpore surrendered to Indian mutineers after a siege. The 78th and 84th Highland regiments then recaptured the town of Cawnpore. When the soldiers went to look for the British residents, what they found horrified them. Most of the captured British men had been massacred and 120 British children and women had been hacked to death with meat cleavers in a small room.

Source 4.45

Colonel John Neill, a Scot, remembered:

'Ladies' and children's bloody torn dresses and shoes were lying about, and locks of hair torn from their heads. The floor of the room they were all dragged into and killed was saturated with blood. One cannot control one's feelings. Who could be merciful to one concerned?'

The Scottish soldiers did not hold back in their revenge. Captured Indian soldiers, and civilians who were not even involved, were forced into the room described above and forced to lick up some of the blood. This was

only ended when Sir Colin Campbell arrived and put a stop to it. However, captured Muslim and Hindu soldiers were humiliated before being put to death. Dreadful acts were committed by both sides.

Source 4.46

The Indian Mutiny reinforced the image of the Scots as a martial race. The image of the Highlander going into action can be seen in this engraving. It was a very powerful and visible image of the Scot abroad.

After the Mutiny was crushed, India remained very important for trade and as a place where Scots served in office and made their fortunes.

Source 4.47

Author Bruce Lenman comments:

'The Scottish middle classes had a substantial interest in the fortunes of the British Empire, especially in India where in the days of the Honourable East India Company Scots had established a tradition of imperial service which survived and flourished when India came directly under the Crown.'

One of the Scotsmen who served in India was Andrew Yule, who arrived in India just after the Indian Mutiny in 1857–8. It was a time of change and industrial development. By the time he arrived the British Government was in direct control of the country. In 1869 the Suez Canal opened between the

Mediterranean and the Red Sea, which led to the Indian Ocean. The canal was known as the 'Highway to India' and created a much faster route from Britain to India. India was also opening up to trade owing to the introduction of railways and the telegraph. One of the first businesses set up by Andrew Yule was with the Hoolungpooree Tea Company. His interest expanded into insurance, cloth companies and, in 1875, into jute. He retired to Britain, a rich man, in 1888. Andrew Yule and Company is an Indian government-owned company even today.

Education, culture and religion

One of the many reasons for the Indian Mutiny was fear of conversion to Christianity. Many Scots came over to India to serve in the religious missions, as they were known. Most Scottish missionaries were well-educated and very keen to educate the Indians. The argument was that if Indians were educated then they would see the truth of God's word in the Bible and help convert the rest of the Indian population. The years after the Mutiny saw an increase in Scottish, and English, missions to India.

No matter what their motives were, the Scottish missionaries had an important role in the development of education in India. One example is the Reverend Alexander Duff. Duff was born in Moulin in Perthshire. He arrived in India in 1830 on a Church of Scotland mission to Calcutta. He opened an educational establishment, which taught in English. Within a week his school had over 300 applicants. He was so successful that his model was used in Bombay, Madras and Nagpur, and his influence was important in the 1854 proposal to establish universities in Calcutta, Bombay and Madras. Duff was particularly linked with helping found the University of Calcutta in 1857, as well as the establishment of the first medical college in the country. This remarkable man is also associated with setting up a number of girls' schools in India.

Other missionaries are also important. John Wilson was from Lauder in Berwickshire. Like Duff he was very interested in education and had a huge influence in Bombay. The educational institution he set up in 1832 was known as the Ambrolie English School and is known today as Wilson College. It is the oldest college in Bombay (now known as Mumbai).

Summary

- Scots made a huge impact on the British Empire as colonists.
- Scots were successful because of their hard work, education and the fact they came from a developed industrial economy.
- Scots influenced the development of the economies across the Empire by becoming politicians, engineers, manufacturers and farmers.

- Scots influenced the development of the education systems of countries in the Empire.
- Scots' religion had an important role across Empire. It was a motive to settle abroad, to work hard and to make contact with native peoples.
- Scots had an effect on the cultures of the Empire by taking with them their own literature, music and games.
- Scots had both good and bad effects on native people. Some Scots were aggressive. Some were supportive and sympathetic.

Activities 

1 Connections

Your job is to make connections between the four countries identified in this chapter – Canada, Australia, New Zealand and India.

Are there similarities or differences in the impact of Scots on different parts of the Empire?

Try to make connections using the following sub-headings to help you.

- Economic growth and development
- Religious and cultural development
- Impact on native societies

There are a number of ways in which you could tackle this task.

- You could work independently and simply make notes using the information in this chapter.
- You could work in a group on ONE of the areas identified above. Your task would be to teach this to the rest of the class and make sure that they have thorough notes and examples.
- You could take one of the themes or countries above and make up a game called 'Find out about the Scots and the Empire economy/ culture/native society'. Make up 20 questions that ask about the topic. Once your classmates have studied the topic try out the quiz. How many marks did they get? Do they need to do more work?
- You could work in pairs and make up a word search to make sure you and your partner know about each topic. Write definitions of your hidden words to help your partner find the words. As they solve your puzzle, you solve theirs!

The choice is yours!

OR

2 Using a large outline map of Canada, Australia, New Zealand or India identify places mentioned in the text on the map. Around this make a note about how and why that place is important for Scots and their impact on the Empire. This will give you a large and visual way of remembering important information about the topic.

5 The effects of migration and Empire on Scotland, to 1939

The immigrant Irish, Jews, Lithuanians and Italians have all contributed to Scotland. This contribution has been largely positive, ranging from helping build a successful economy before the war to broadening the ways in which Scots spent their spare time.

Scotland's importance in developing the Empire also saw changes within Scotland. The Empire was a very important market for Scottish products as well as the source of much raw material for Scottish industry. The Empire was a place that Scots found jobs in. Many returned to Scotland after their time abroad. They brought home money that was invested in Scotland, as well as new habits and customs. The Empire was also of great importance in developing Scotland's own sense of identity. Scottish soldiers fought with great skill abroad, especially in India where the distinctive appearance of the Highland Regiments helped to build Scotland's reputation as a martial nation.

The contribution of immigrants to Scottish society, economy and culture

The contribution of the Irish

The importance of Irish immigrants to Scotland has been commented on by numerous historians.

Source 5.1

Tom Devine states:

'The immigration of the Irish into Scotland forms one of the most significant themes of modern Scottish history. The movement transformed the population of several lowland towns but especially Glasgow, Greenock, Dundee, Paisley, Coatbridge and Motherwell and Airdrie, among others. Scotland's industrialisation was helped because employers had access to a huge pool of Irish labour which was not only cheap but, equally important, was very mobile and adaptable. The huge construction schemes of the nineteenth-century cities and the building of roads, railways, canals, docks and harbours depended on this vast labour supply. The immigration was concentrated in particular parts of the country, more especially the western Lowlands but also in Dundee and, to a lesser extent, Edinburgh.'

The immigrant Irish had a positive economic effect on Scotland. The Irish labourers were prepared to tackle the hardest of jobs. There would have been few industrial developments in Scotland without them. They contributed to the building of roads, canals and railways across Scotland and the rest of Britain. There are a couple of examples of the importance of the Irish in developing the transport, which allowed the Scottish economy to grow. In February 1847, a total of 6245 navvies were employed to build the Edinburgh and Northern Railway line in Fife: 4103 of these workers were Scots, 2110 Irish and only 32 English. Similarly, in the 1890s, the Glasgow Subway was tunnelled and built largely by the use of Irish immigrant labour. Some historians believed that, without the Irish, the industrial revolution would never have been as successful as it was in Britain.

The descendants of Irish immigrants also had a positive effect on Scotland. Thomas Lipton's father was a poor Irish immigrant who worked in a Glasgow mill, saved up his money and bought a small grocer's shop with his hard-earned cash. After emigrating to America when he was just 15 years old, Thomas returned to Glasgow aged 20 where he opened his first shop selling reasonably priced groceries. By the age of 30 he was a millionaire, famous for his Lipton's tea and chain of shops. He died in 1931 and is buried in the family mausoleum in Glasgow's Southern Necropolis.

Source 5.2

An advertisement for Lipton's tea from 1892.

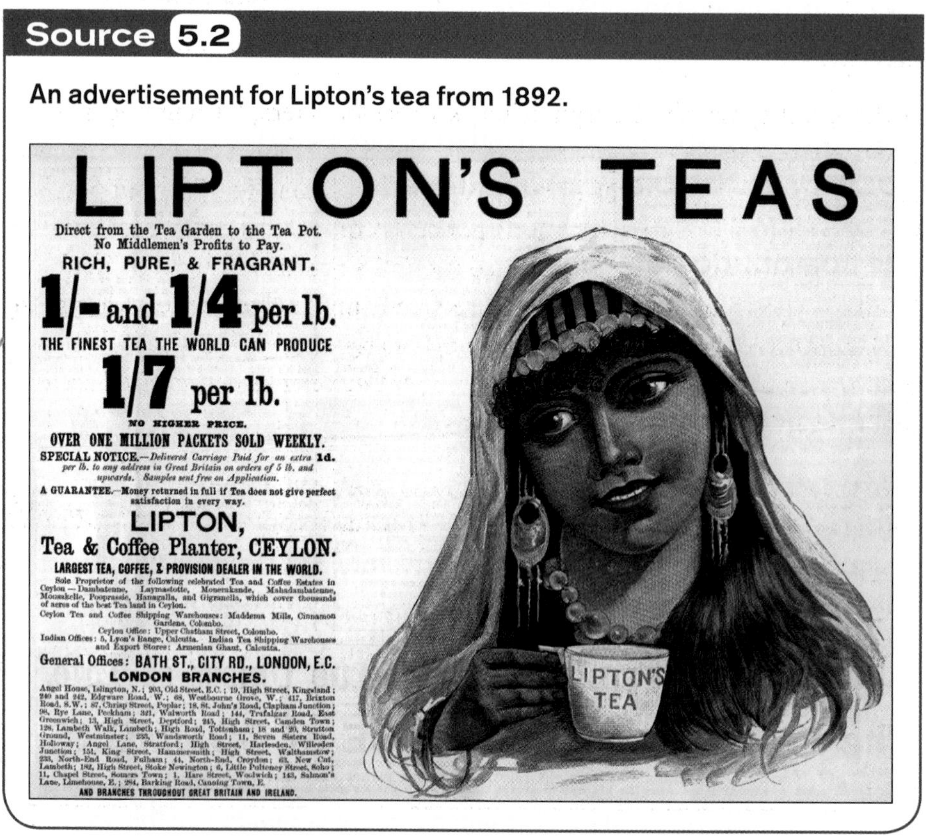

Cultural impact

The Irish had a lasting cultural impact on Scottish society in the development of a school system that has separate Catholic schools across most major urban centres in Scotland. There has also been a lasting contribution to the sporting life of Scotland through football clubs that were set up by the Irish Catholic community. Edinburgh Hibernian was founded in 1875 by Irishmen living in the Cowgate area of Edinburgh. There were so many Irish living in the Cowgate that it was known as 'Little Ireland'. Glasgow Celtic was founded in 1887 by Brother Walfrid, a Catholic priest. Although there had been a Catholic team in Dundee called Dundee Harp, it folded in 1879. Dundee United was founded in 1909 and was originally called Dundee Hibernian. Other contributions of the Irish to the culture of Scotland can be seen through the Protestant Orange Lodge Order. It has added a distinctive element to Scottish culture through their annual parades.

Source 5.3

Edinburgh Hibernian badge: the harp shows the importance of the Irish to the club.

Although they first had a reputation as strike-breakers, Irish immigrants and their descendants were important in the Scottish trade union movement and the development of the Labour Party in Scotland. The Irish supported the Labour Party because Labour's policies promised to deal with issues like poor housing and also supported the 1918 Scottish Education Act. Similarly they got involved in organised trade unions because of a common need among both Irish and Scottish workers for a living wage and safe working conditions. The historian John McCaffrey has commented on a real Irish influence in setting up unions.

Source 5.4

John McCaffrey states:

'The National Labourers Union which catered for building trades labourers was very Irish both in direction and membership in Glasgow. Irish elements were prominent, too, in the development of a Union catering for Glasgow Corporation employees in the later nineteenth and early twentieth centuries.'

Source 5.5

John Wheatley

The Irish community produced important political leaders like John Wheatley and James Connelly as well.

John Wheatley was born in Ireland in 1869. His family moved to Scotland in 1876. He worked as a miner and became very involved in left-wing politics. He joined the Independent Labour Party (ILP) in 1907 and was heavily involved in campaigns against conscription and rent rises in Glasgow during the First World War. He was elected as a councillor, before being elected as an MP in 1922 for the Glasgow Shettleston seat. By this stage the ILP was part of the Labour Party. When the Labour Party formed a government in 1924, Wheatley was made Minister of Health. He is perhaps best remembered for a Housing Act in 1924 which saw the building of affordable housing for working-class men and women. Approximately 500,000 houses were built under his scheme, which provided subsidies of money to encourage local councils to build such housing. Wheatley was a devout Catholic all his life. He died in 1930.

Source 5.6

James Connelly

James Connelly was the son of Irish immigrants. He was born in the Cowgate area of Edinburgh in 1868. He worked as a labourer and served for a brief time in the British Army. He became involved in left-wing politics when living in Dundee. He became secretary of the Scottish Socialist Federation and worked closely with the Independent Labour Party, before moving to Ireland in 1896. Connelly came to believe in an independent, socialist Ireland free from British rule. In 1912 he founded the Irish Labour Party. He is perhaps most famous for his leadership role with the Irish Citizens Army and their involvement in the 1916 Easter Rising in Dublin against British rule of Ireland. Connelly was shot by the British, along with 14 others, after the surrender of those involved in the Rising. Because of an injury to his ankle, he could not stand up, so he was tied to a chair before facing the firing squad.

The Irish are the most numerous and significant immigrant community in Scotland. Their importance to the economic and cultural development of Scotland cannot be underestimated.

The contribution of Italians, Jews and Lithuanians

Italians

The Italian contribution to Scottish society has been both visible and welcome!

Source 5.7

Joe Pieri sums up what the Italians brought with them to Scotland:

'The well-appointed ice-cream shops that developed from the ice-cream barrows once pushed through the streets by these immigrants added a new dimension to the leisure life of the youth of Scotland, and provided them with a place to congregate and meet. Fish and chip shops matched the growth of the cafes and provided the working classes with a cheap and nourishing meal which grew to be a staple of their diet.'

Source 5.8

Italian ice-cream shop in Edinburgh, 1907

Italian families contributed to the growing leisure industry. The growth of cafes is an example of this. In 1903 there were 89 cafes in Glasgow; there were 336 cafes by 1905. Italian families settled in many towns on the coast and in the main cities. In Largs, the Nardini family developed what was to become the largest cafe in Britain! Nardini's had a glass-lined ice-cream mixer and the first soda-fountain seen in Britain. The 'Costa del Glasgow' had been born. The Italians did not just open up cafes. An Italian food and wine business, R. Valvona and Co., was established in Edinburgh in the 1900s, and Alfonso Crolla joined the company in 1934. They opened up a delicatessen on Elm Row in Edinburgh, and the famous Valvona and Crolla was born. Small towns like Lossiemouth on the Moray Firth also boasted their own Italian cafes.

Source 5.9

Italian cafe in Eyemouth

As the Italian community became wealthier, organisations emerged that added to the style of Scotland. In the late 1920s, for example, the College of Italian Hairdressers was set up in Glasgow.

Source 5.10

Joe Pieri sums up the story of the Italians in Scotland:

'The history of the Italians in Scotland is a story of what can be achieved by people of lowly and underprivileged beginnings, with little or no education, and with nothing to rely on except their own inner strength and determination to survive and prosper, so as to provide for their families a future which they could not hope for in the land of their birth. It is also a story of how immigrants can enrich and bring a new dimension and flavour to the customs and culture of their adopted land.'

Jews

Jewish immigrants helped to develop the commercial life of Scotland. Their involvement in the tobacco industry and tailoring trade was important, for example. As the Jewish community grew wealthier, they moved from places like the Gorbals in Glasgow to the more fashionable West End. The community also increasingly sought jobs in professions like medicine.

Source 5.11

Jewish-owned tobacco shop in Glasgow, before 1903

One major impact of the immigrant community was the creation of a new industry in Scotland. There was no local workforce that could produce cigarettes, so Jacob Kramrisch, the Austrian-born Jewish manager of the Imperial Tobacco Company in Glasgow from 1888, recruited his workers directly from Jewish tobacco workplaces in Hamburg in Germany and Warsaw in Poland. Cigarette making was a common job for Jewish immigrants to Scotland. When he gave evidence about the immigration of Jewish workers, to a Royal Commission on Alien Immigration in 1903, Kramrisch told not only of the new industry had been created in Glasgow, but also of how well it competed with American competition, and how it had attracted other tobacco manufacturers to Glasgow, creating yet more jobs.

Perhaps the other major impact of the Jewish community was to make the average Scot better dressed at affordable prices. Julius Pinto, a Jewish tailor, gave evidence to the Commission mentioned above and said that not only was crime low in Jewish areas of Glasgow, but the Jews had made suits cheaper with more efficient methods of production: whereas a Scottish worker created the whole suit, the Jewish tailors had organised themselves through what was called piece-work, making parts of the suit before it was assembled. This enabled the Jewish tailors to produce a quality suit at a cheap price. As a result, ready-made suits had become much more widely available in Scotland by the early twentieth century.

Source 5.12

Dr Kenneth Collins comments:

'The influx of Jews to Glasgow had promoted trading opportunities and thus employment and had not taken work from native Scots.'

Lithuanians

The impact of the Lithuanian community added to the economic development of Scotland in that they were workers in the coal-mining industry. They also added a distinctive culture to Scotland with their language and community activities. However, as noted in Chapter 2, the Lithuanian community integrated very effectively into Scottish society so there is far less of a lasting legacy. With the emergence of the First World War many returned to Eastern Europe.

Source 5.13

Female Lithuanian mine workers in Carfin, Lanarkshire, in 1919

The impact of the Empire on Scotland

In the years before the First World War the wealth of trade and the Empire transformed many urban centres in Scotland. Glasgow in these years was at the peak of its self-confidence. By the 1880s fine classical buildings had been constructed in the city centre. Such buildings were a sign of the

confidence that the Empire and wealth brought to the city. By 1921 Glasgow was referring to itself as the 'second city of the Empire'.

Dundee is also an excellent example of the impact made on Scotland by the Empire: materials from the Empire were combined with work skills in Scotland to create more money. The East India Company sent samples of jute to Britain to see if the fibre could be used. Jute came from Bengal in India and was a very coarse vegetable fibre, but it was cheap and it was hoped that it could be used to produce fabric of some sort. The problem of dealing with this dry and brittle fibre was solved in Dundee. The city was an important whaling centre and one product of this was whale oil. Dundee was also a centre of linen production and so had expertise in producing cloth. When raw jute was softened with whale oil and water it became useable in a product commonly called hessian. This cloth is used for things like sacks. The connection between Dundee, India and the jute industry was born.

The historian Tom Devine has commented on how the Scottish economy expanded largely due to the demands of the export market. Much of this production went to the British Empire, though not all.

Source 5.14

Tom Devine comments:

'The new industrial and urban society depended on a number of important factors. Most importantly, the economy relied overwhelmingly upon access to overseas markets. Some 38 per cent of all Scottish coal production went abroad in the 1910s... The giant North British Locomotive Company sent nearly half its engines to the British Empire in the years before the First World War, with India as the primary destination. The rise of Dundee jute was generated from the 1840s by the demand for bags for international commodities as varied as East India coffee and Latin-American guano. The ships that poured out from the yards of Clydeside relied for orders on the condition of international trade... It was the same story everywhere, from quality Border knitwear to malt and blended whiskies. As far as Scotland was concerned, the international market was the king.'

The example of the locomotive industry shows how important the Empire and export were to the Scottish economy. Locomotive production was an important industry for Scotland. Workshops that produced locomotives existed from Inverurie in Aberdeenshire to Glasgow. In Glasgow, really large companies developed. In 1903 three independent Glasgow-based railway engine building companies formed one company called the North British Locomotive Works. This company could produce 800 locomotives every year. It was the largest centre of railway engine production in Europe. Engines were exported across the Empire as well as to places like South America. The company produced one quarter of the steam locomotives used by New Zealand Railways and supplied large numbers to Canada and India as well.

Source 5.15

Royal train, climbing the Rimutaka Incline, New Zealand, 1930s

Source 5.16

Workshop of the Empire: the loading of a YP class 4-8-0 locomotive on board a cargo ship at Finnieston docks in Glasgow, destined for India.

The other large industry which really benefited from the Empire was shipbuilding. Owing to Scottish innovations such as the design of a more efficient engine for ships, steam ships became competitive on the long trade routes from Britain to India and beyond. The Clyde became the centre of this industry as it was close to sources of iron and coal for steel production, as well as having a skilled workforce. Between 1851 and 1870 the Clyde produced an impressive 70 per cent of iron ships made in Britain!

Source 5.17

Advertisement for Fairfield's Shipbuilding works

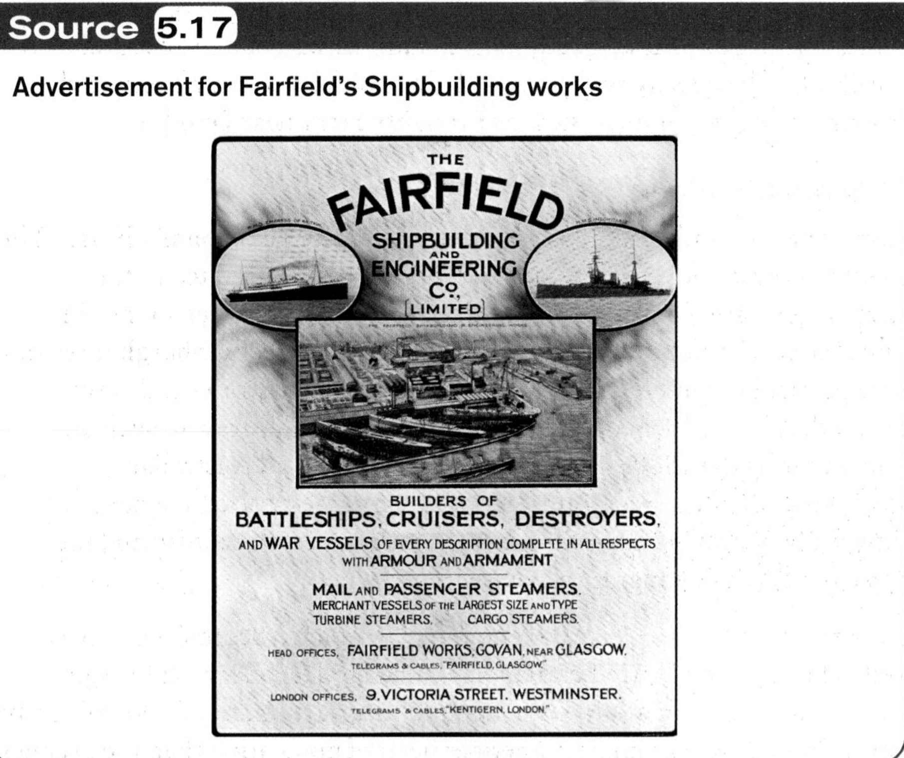

Shipyards like Fairfield's, Beardmore's and Denny's were world leaders in the production of shipping in the years up to 1914. They provided the transport that linked the British Empire together.

Source 5.18

The importance of the Empire to Scottish industry is summed up by Bruce Lenman:

'The wheat of the Canadian or American prairies, for example, had to be taken by rail to eastern ports, and in Canada the locomotive could well be made in Glasgow while both in Canada and in America the sacks holding the grain were quite likely to have been manufactured in Dundee. The ships which crossed the North Atlantic with the grain were often enough built and engineered on the Clyde.'

Wealth

A handful of families made huge fortunes from the profits of the export industries that serviced the Empire and beyond. Before 1914, Scottish businessmen like Sir Charles Tenant (chemicals), Sir James and Peter Coats (cotton thread) and William Weir (coal and iron) were thought to be worth more than £2 million.

However, this wealth can also be seen in the growth of a confident middle class who invested money abroad and in their own living arrangements at home. The middle classes had grown to number 267,300 in Scotland by the late 1860s. The display of their wealth and confidence can be seen in the growth of elegant suburbs, such as Broughty Ferry near Dundee.

Investment abroad and at home

Scots were also willing to invest money (also known as capital) abroad. This investment was a feature after 1870 and was probably related to the increasing wealth of the Scottish middle class. Scots invested money in America mostly, but also in the Empire. Aberdeen and Edinburgh investors were particularly interested in the development of Australia and New Zealand. After 1870, Scottish investment in Australia grew to such an extent that by the 1880s no less than 40 per cent of all Australian borrowing was from Scotland. This confirmed the close connection between Scotland's economic success in the nineteenth century and the impact of Scottish emigration overseas.

Investments in India, Sri Lanka and Burma attracted Scottish capital as well. The historian Bruce Lenman has calculated that Scottish foreign investment rose from £60 million in 1870 to approximately £500 million by 1914. This figure was much higher per head of population than the average for the United Kingdom as a whole.

Money from the Empire helped some landed families who were struggling in Scotland's rural economy. One example of this is from the north-east of Scotland where the Forbes family of Newe had owned a country estate since the sixteenth century. The estate benefited from connections with India as the family became merchants in India. The estate was sold, but was repurchased with the fortune made by Alasdair Forbes in India. The House of Forbes in Bombay produced a flow of money which allowed the Forbes family in Aberdeenshire to invest in land improvements and even to buy neighbouring properties and expand in the Strathdon area.

The opportunities offered by the Empire were also important to many ordinary households in Scotland. Many Scots travelled abroad to make money and then came home again with the money they made, although not all of them became wealthy. In many cases the money made abroad made an important contribution to the local economy.

Source 5.19

Marjorie Harper comments:

'Arctic earnings were a vital part of the household economy of many sojourners' [temporary migrants'] wives and parents and also helped to stimulate trade in the Northern and Western Isles.'

Money found its way to Scotland from across the Empire. It was wealth from India that funded the development of Dr Gray's Hospital and the Anderson Institute, both in Elgin, for example. However, the Empire offered a range of opportunities, not just that of becoming a successful businessman.

Source 5.20

Marjory Harper states:

'India was a place where younger sons of the Scottish gentry and merchant classes sought their fortunes as well as a field of service for recently created Highland regiments.'

The martial tradition

The Empire helped create the reputation of the Scot as an effective soldier. Interestingly the image that was created was firmly centred on the Highlands of Scotland (see Source 5.21).

Source 5.21

Ewan Cameron comments:

'The Indian rebellion of 1857 was the site of a renewed emphasis on the tradition of Highlanders as a martial race.'

The historian Hew Strachan has pointed out that the nineteenth century saw a drop in the numbers of Scots, in particular Highlanders, serving in the British Army. This was understandable owing to emigration and the decline in the Highland population. He states that in 1830 Scots were 10 per cent of the population of Britain, but over 13 per cent of the army. By 1870, Scots were 10.5 per cent of the British population, but only 8 per cent of the army. Scottish soldiers were therefore not a very important part of the British Army in terms of numbers. Their importance was a result of their image. The image of the Highland soldier was very important in Victorian Britain.

Source 5.22

Hew Strachan comments:

'The warrior image of the Highlands proved both powerful and resilient. It saved Scotland's military identity just when it ought to have been ended. Highlanders hogged the limelight in the great imperial sagas of the 1850s. In 1857 the beleaguered garrison at Lucknow [besieged during the Indian mutiny], Scottish women among them, had their first sign of relief when they heard the approaching bagpipes of Sir Colin Campbell's column. The Highlander became the defender of the Empire.'

As mentioned in Chapter 4, the Scots provided leadership and many of the soldiers during the Indian Mutiny. In Scotland, the 'Highland craze', as it was known, meant that even Lowland regiments were wearing tartan and had pipe bands by the end of the nineteenth century. The Highland identity had become the Scottish identity. The Highland craze of the nineteenth century was partly due to the novels of Sir Walter Scott, but was also to do with Queen Victoria. She and her husband bought Balmoral Castle in Scotland as a private estate in 1847. The royal family went to Highland games and dressed in Highland dress. As a result, a particular view of the Highlands became very popular. This can be seen in the development of a Highland/Scottish military identity. Of course the reality was that the Highlands could not supply enough men for the army. Most of the 'Scottish' part of the British Army was recruited in the towns of the Lowlands during the nineteenth and early twentieth centuries. However, the way in which the Highland image spread is understandable. Newspapers from the time liked the stories and the images. Dressing in tartan and wearing the kilt made Scottish soldiers stand out in a distinctive way as the images below show.

Source 5.23

The charge of the Highlanders before Cawnpore, under General Havelock, during the Indian Mutiny of 1857. Engraving from 1858.

Source 5.24

The Highland soldier in a martial pose: such images reinforced the image of the Scottish soldier as a Highland soldier.

India has also had a very interesting role in developing language in Britain. Words learned in India came back to Scotland and are in common use here. The example of 'thug' has been mentioned in a previous chapter. The word 'bungalow' means a house in the Bengal style. Bengal was where British families would go when the heat became too much on the plains of India. Bengal was in the north and had a cooler climate. A bungalow was a single-level shelter with a sloping roof. Other examples of words that come from the days of the Empire are 'avatar', 'loot' and 'pyjamas'.

Competition from the Empire

Developments in the Empire had an impact on the Scottish economy from the end of the nineteenth century. A concentration on heavy engineering and fabric production for export markets had created great wealth in Scotland. Scots abroad helped the economies to develop in countries such as Australia and Canada. But by doing this Scots contributed to economic problems that would hit Scotland and Britain in the years leading up to and after the First World War.

Once areas of the Empire developed their own agriculture and industry they became serious competitors for Scottish producers. In particular, Scottish agriculture was affected by the arrival of chilled and frozen beef and mutton from Australia after 1870. It was even a Scottish emigrant who was behind the first successful shipment of refrigerated meat!

The First World War saw a boom in Scottish industry. The heavy industry was perfectly placed for large-scale armaments production. Dundee's jute mills also worked hard producing sand-bags as well as tent material. However, when the war ended, this concentration on particular heavy industries became a serious problem for Scotland. Traditional overseas markets like Australia had been lost as America had stepped in to fill the gap caused by the loss of Scottish products during the war.

Foreign investment by Scottish entrepreneurs also caused problems. For example, Margaret Donnelly, a jute mill landowner in Dundee in the 1800s, set up the first jute mills in Bengal. By 1914 Bengal jute mills were making huge profits based on the very low wages paid to its Indian workers. Prices and demand for jute fell after 1920. The great economic depression of 1929 also had an effect. Employment levels in the jute industry in Scotland fell from 35,000 workers to 26,000 workers between 1929 and 1939. Most of these workers were women. Price competition from India also effectively finished off what was left of the cotton industry in Glasgow and the west of Scotland by the end of the 1920s. India had even started to build its own railway engines by 1895.

Bruce Lenman sums up the factors that had made Scottish industry great in the years before 1914, but were to form its problems after 1919 (Source 5.25).

Source 5.25

Bruce Lenman states:

'Scotland's failure between 1921 and 1939 was primarily a failure to attract or develop new industry. In the period 1930–9, with a major world depression and consequent collapse of world trade, it is difficult to imagine a more vulnerable regional economy than the heavy capital goods, export-orientated type which Scotland had inherited.'

Summary

- Immigrant people made a significant contribution to the economic, social and cultural development of Scotland.
- Access to the British Empire helped the Scottish economy grow in the years leading up to the First World War. In particular, the locomotive, jute and shipbuilding industries developed.
- Individual Scots became very wealthy as a result of trade with the Empire and beyond.
- The Empire was also important as a place for Scots to work and invest money.

- The Empire was important in contributing to the image of the Scot as a good soldier. The image of the Scottish soldier became identified with that of the Highlander.
- By the twentieth century the Empire had become a competitor to many Scottish industries.

Activities

1 Work in pairs.

- One person take the topic of the effect of migration on Scotland.
- One person take the topic of the effect of the Empire on Scotland.

Read this chapter and make a note of all the ways Scotland was affected in relation to your topic. You will need to find at least **ten** for each topic.

You now have to teach your partner your topic. Decide what the most important effects were and give reasons why you think this. Think of ways to make the topic interesting for your partner. Do not just provide a list of notes. Use various activities. For example, you could:

- make up a quiz
- make up a large word search with clues
- make up a spider diagram, using visuals/pictures for each of the effects you have identified.

Be creative!

How will you know you have been successful in your teaching?

2 Reinforce your skills by looking at past examination questions on Issue 4 (the impact of Scots emigrants on the growth and development of the Empire). Can you make up marking schemes by using the information you have learnt? If you can, then you have learnt the relevant information and have managed to remember it. Congratulations.

6 Perspective

The period from 1830 to 1939 saw events that had a big effect on the 'image' or 'identity' of Scotland in the world. The effects of emigration and immigration led to major changes in the way Scots thought about Scotland, and what the rest of the world thought about Scotland.

Scottish identity and emigration

Even today, for many people the identity of Scots and Scotland in the nineteenth century is linked to thoughts of romantic Highlanders being forced from their homes by heartless landowners. This is the 'victim' identity of Scotland and it was an identity created by writers and artists throughout the nineteenth century – but is it true?

Source 6.1

This painting by Thomas Faed is called *The Last of the Clan*. It was painted in 1865. When this painting was exhibited in London, barriers had to be set out to control the crowd. The romantic picture of a noble people forced to emigrate because of greedy landlords was a powerful one and is still with us today.

This interpretation of Scottish history and emigration is partly true when applied to events in the Western Highlands. However, it is not the whole story as far as Scotland is concerned. Emigration happened for many reasons but few of those reasons were dramatic enough to be 'front page news' – or the subject of paintings. Most Scottish emigrants came from the Lowlands of Scotland. However, stories of Scots leaving to follow family or to become richer are just not as dramatic or confrontational. This is why emigration is forever linked to events in the Highlands of Scotland, as Source 6.2 reinforces.

Source 6.2

Like *The Last of the Clan* in source 6.1, *Lochaber No More*, painted in 1883, used the departure from the Highlands as its subject.

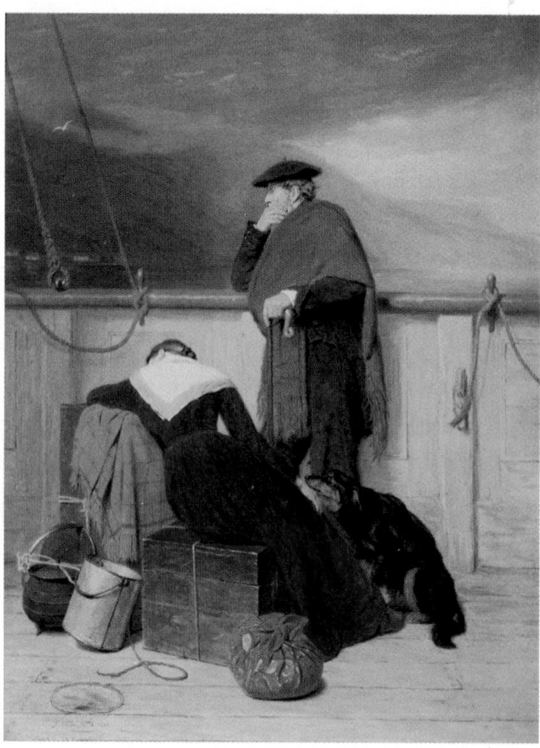

The common view of Scottish emigration is that of emigration forced on a reluctant people.

Scottish identity abroad

As Scots emigrated they took an identity with them. All too often this meant an identity from the Highlands of Scotland. In many ways this was understandable. For many Highland emigrants there was bitterness at the way in which they had been forced or encouraged to leave. The historian Michael Lynch has commented on how this had an effect on countries that Scots settled in.

Source 6.3

Michael Lynch states:

'In Canada especially, the mass shipment of whole communities helped to preserve a folk memory of the Clearances, which had brought them to where they were. In Australia, which was to a far greater extent the destination of emigrants from the eastern Lowlands, the sense of a whole community uprooted was much slighter.'

Even Lowlanders joined in with the common view of what an emigrant Scot was like. New Zealand is a good example of this. The majority of Scottish emigrants to New Zealand were from the Lowlands of Scotland. This means that most were from the industrial and urbanised parts of Scotland centred on Glasgow and Edinburgh. However, when they arrived in places like Otago and Southland they created an image of Scotland that had nothing to do with the Scotland they had left.

Source 6.4

Writers Jock Philips and Terry Hearn state:

'From the mid-1860s Caledonian societies were established in most small communities of Otago and Southland, and in other parts of the country. These operated partly as charitable institutions, but they also deliberately fostered Scots culture. They taught Scots literature and history, and held Caledonian Games which encouraged Highland traditions such as the playing of bagpipes and Highland dancing.'

Such traditions were also kept alive by an active press.

Source 6.5

The New Zealand *Scotsman* magazine, published between 1912 and 1933. It helped keep Scottish traditions alive.

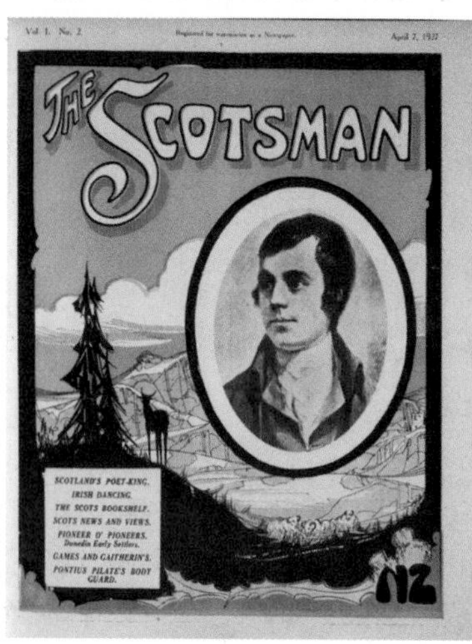

Source 6.6

The Cameron family of Mataura. The 'invented' Highland tradition of kilts, pipe bands, dancing and games that defined Scottish identity in New Zealand can be seen in this photograph. Kenneth Cameron founded New Zealand's first civilian pipe band in 1896.

Scots' setting up a new home abroad tended to be even more 'Scottish' than those at home.

Source 6.7

Historian Michael Lynch comments:

'A settler patriotism produced Caledonian societies, Burns Clubs and Highland Gatherings in greater numbers than in Scotland. It was in this Greater Scotland overseas that a form of Scottishness – freed from the complexities of living in a nation within a larger nation-state – flourished most.'

Scottish identity and immigration

Immigrants had an important effect on Scottish identity. The most important group were the immigrant Irish, Catholic and Protestant. Their influence on political, educational, religious and cultural life in Scotland was and is very important. This is particularly true in the west of Scotland, but can also be seen in Edinburgh and Dundee. Other immigrant groups, such as Jewish and Italian people, kept their distinct identities within Scottish culture. Others, like the Lithuanians, have largely disappeared. Although it is always risky to generalise about large numbers of people who chose to either leave or arrive in Scotland, it is true that migration had made Scotland a more complex, culturally rich place in 1939 than it had been in 1830.

Scottish identity: the importance of the Empire

If the Empire and the 'Highland craze' had saved or even created the reputation of the Scottish soldier it was to be the First World War that saw mass volunteering for the British Army by Scots. Scots also affirmed their identity as British subjects and defenders of the Empire. This was certainly true in the years up to the end of the First World War, and it had important results.

Source 6.8

Historian Hew Strachan states:

'With the outbreak of the First World War, Scots joined up at a greater rate than did men from England, Wales and Ireland. By July 1915 the average rate of enlistment for all males in Britain was 20 per cent, but in Scotland it was 24 per cent. Many Scots joined up out of economic necessity. But Scots now acted out of their warrior identity, and in doing so confirmed identification with the Empire.'

Politically, there was no widespread desire for an independent Scotland in the years up to 1919. The fact was that their role in the Empire gave Scots an important role within Britain. Scottish soldiers were seen as the shock troops of the Empire, who could be called on in times of trouble. Scottish administrators managed the Empire. It has been calculated that one third of colonial Governor-Generals between 1850 and 1939 were Scots.

Being Scottish meant status and opportunity. To the average Scot there was nothing wrong with being proud of Scotland, proud of Britain and proud of the Empire.

Economically, the Empire shaped Scotland. It provided careers for Scots abroad. It drove Scottish industrial development in the nineteenth century. The Empire provided markets for goods made in Scotland. Scotland was known as the 'workshop of the Empire' and Glasgow as the 'second city of the Empire'.

The last words belong to Scottish historian Tom Devine.

Source 6.9

Tom Devine comments:

'So intense was the Scottish engagement with Empire that it affected almost every nook and cranny of Scottish life: industrialisation, intellectual activity, politics, identity, education, popular culture, consumerism, labour markets, demographic trends, Highland social development and much else. In a word, Empire was fundamental to the moulding of the Scottish nation.'

Activities 

1 Your challenge is to produce a display or presentation showing the effects of migration and the Empire on Scotland's identity. Your display or presentation must make people want to stop and look at your conclusions about these effects.

Your teacher will give you an appropriate amount of time to complete the task.

Work in groups of no more than four.

Your display or presentation must cover the following topics:

- Effects of emigration on Scotland's identity
- Effects of immigration on Scotland's identity
- Effects of the Empire on Scotland's identity

continued 

Success criteria

There is a huge amount of information on these topics so you must be selective in deciding what you and your group think is important.

- Select at least six pieces of important evidence for each of the three topics.
- In your presentation there must be at least one illustration for each of the three topics.
- Make the presentation colourful, and use slogans or catch phrases for each of the three topics.

2 **Extended writing exercise**. Work in groups of three. Choose one of these essay titles for your group:

- How important was emigration in shaping Scottish national identity?
- How far was Scottish identity shaped by immigration?
- 'The Empire was important in shaping Scottish national identity.' How valid is this view?

Your job is to make up an essay plan for your group's chosen essay title. Each person in the group should make up their own essay plan.

- Decide how many paragraphs you will have in the essay.
- Decide what the theme or topic of each paragraph will be.
- For each paragraph state two facts you would include.
- For each paragraph outline an opinion on that issue. Remember to link this to the essay question you have chosen.

Your group now has three essay plans. Compare them and see what they have in common and what is different about them.

- Is the information you are using the same?
- How does the comment or argument differ?

Preparing for Paper 2 of the Higher History Exam

Paper 2 of your Higher History exam is based entirely on source analysis. The exam paper will be divided into five special topics. This book is about **ONE** of those special topics: Migration and Empire, 1830–1939.

What will paper 2 of my exam be about?

You will have to answer ONE special topic section. You must answer all of the questions set on the special topic you have studied.

There will be questions on other special topics that other candidates have studied. Make sure you answer the correct special topic.

Your special topic syllabus is divided into six main sections. Check out the Arrangements document on the SQA website at **http://www.sqa.org.uk**. There you will find the detailed content for the special topic 'Migration and Empire, 1830–1939'.

The first section you will see is called 'Background'. The last section is called 'Perspective'. Neither of those sections will have any questions asked about them. They are **NOT** examined. That leaves four other sections, called issues, and each of these issues has a question linked to it.

What do I have to do?

You will have five sources to use and four questions to answer. You will have 1 hour and 25 minutes to do that. That means you will have about 20 minutes to deal with each question so answers must be well structured and well developed. Put simply, that means you must do three things for each question:

1. **You must do what you are asked to do.**
2. **You must refer to information in the source(s).**
3. **You must also include your own relevant recalled information when asked to do so.**

Each question also has its own particular process that you must use to answer the question successfully. Later in this section there are sample answers to show you how to deal with the different questions.

What types of questions will I be asked?

There are FOUR different types of question. Each type will be asked ONCE in your exam paper.

Important: In this book the questions are listed as Type 1, 2, 3 and 4. This does **NOT** mean the questions will appear in that order in the exam. The different types of question can appear in **ANY** order.

Question Type 1 is a Source Evaluation Question worth 5 Marks.

The question will ask 'How useful is Source A in explaining/as evidence of...?'

In this type of question you are being asked to judge how good the source is as a piece of historical evidence.

- You will get up to a maximum of 2 marks for commenting in detail about the source's origin (who wrote it or where the source first appeared) and its purpose (why the source was produced).
- You will only get up to 1 mark by identifying and commenting briefly on where the source is from and why it was produced.
- For 2 marks you will be expected to explain why the parts of the source you have selected are useful in terms of the question.

You will get up to a maximum of 2 marks for explaining why the parts of the source you have selected are useful in terms of the question:

- There are no marks for just copying chunks of the source.
- Just listing relevant points from the source will only gain 1 mark.
- For 2 marks you must mention a point from the source and ALSO explain why the evidence you have selected is relevant to the question.
- Watch out for how that works in the examples that follow.

You will get up to a maximum of 2 marks for using your own detailed knowledge as long as it is relevant to the question. This is called using relevant recall:

- You might, for example, want to consider if the source is entirely useful. A source will seldom be entirely valuable or useful. It will have limitations and it is up to you to explain what are the limits to its usefulness.
- In this case a useful word to use is 'partly'.
- You can give evidence to show that the source has its uses, but also include information to suggest the source does not give the whole picture.

This looks like the total number of marks available for the question comes to 6, but there is only a possible total of 5 marks for the question. Stop to think how this helps you. If you had a weak section on origin and purpose you might only get 1 mark out of 2. But if your other two sections are well done, gaining the maximum of 2 marks per part, then you can still achieve the maximum total of 5 marks.

Question type 2 is a Comparison Question worth 5 Marks.

You will be asked to compare two points of view overall and in detail.

The wording of the question will be as follows: 'To what extent do Sources B and C agree about...?'

You will get up to a maximum of **2 marks** for an **overall comparison**. That means you should outline the main differences or agreements identified in the two sources.

You will get up to a maximum of **4 marks** by **developing** your comparison in **detail**.

To get all **4 marks** it is *not enough* just to list points of difference between the sources. In fact you will get **NO MARKS** for simply stating 'Source B says... but Source C says...'

- You **MUST** show that you understand the points made in the source and explain in what ways they differ from each other or support each other.
- When you are explaining the differences or similarities it can be a good idea to use your own detailed knowledge to support your answer.
- There will always be **4** points of comparison for you to find in the sources.
- You will get **NO MARKS** for 'ghost' comparisons. In other words, no marks for writing 'Source B says... but Source C makes no mention of this'.

Question Type 3 is a 'How far...' Question and is worth 10 Marks.

This question is to test your knowledge on one specific part of an issue, called a sub-issue. You can find all the sub-issues in the Specimen Question Paper on the SQA syllabus website at the following address: **http://www.sqa.org.uk/sqa/files_ccc/History%20Higher%20Specimen%202011.pdf.**

A question that asks 'How far does Source B explain the factors that forced Scots to leave Scotland?' tests your knowledge of the factors, or reasons, why Scots were forced to leave their country.

To answer this question you must show that you have **understood the factors** why Scots were forced to leave their country that are included in the source. Take care when doing this as sources can have extra information that is not relevant to the question. It is therefore very important that you read the question carefully before you select the relevant information from the source. You must be able to explain these factors' relevance to the question. You can get up to **4 marks** by identifying and explaining the four significant views that are in the source.

In order to get full marks you must make a judgement and balance the source with **your own accurate and relevant knowledge**. No source will give you the entire answer to a 'How far...' question. Therefore, showing that you understand that there were other reasons that forced Scots to leave that are not included in the source, and explaining these, is vital if you want to get a good mark. You can get up to **7 marks** for this part of your answer.

Question Type 4 is a 'How fully...' Question and is worth 10 Marks.

This question is to test your knowledge of a whole issue. Remember there are four issues in the syllabus that will be examined.

The question could ask 'How fully does Source C explain the impact of Scots emigrants on the Empire?' This relates to Issue 3 from the syllabus.

Just as in the other 10 mark question, you can get up to 4 marks for explaining the points in the source relevant to the question. You can then get up to **7 marks** for relevant **detailed recall** that helps answer the question directly by identifying areas not covered by the presented source.

Now do some training!

Read this before you start answering questions. It will help you to improve your answers.

Activities 

1 After each worked example you will see another question for you to try yourself. Read again the advice about writing a good answer.

2 Write your answer.

3 Exchange your answer with a partner. Use the information you have about how marks are given to judge the value of your partner's answer. Return the marked answer. If there is any disagreement or difficulty ask your teacher to referee!

4 Once you have agreed the final mark take time to think about why you got the mark you did. Make two columns. Title one column 'What I did well'. Title the other column 'What I could improve on'. Use the feedback from your partner, your teacher and your own thoughts about your mark to complete the columns. Next time you do these types of question remember these columns!

The reason for doing this exercise is to understand and use the mark scheme. Once you know how marks are given you can structure your own answers to provide what markers are looking for.

Question type 1 – Source Evaluation

Here is an example of a source evaluation question.

Source A is a poster advertising for men who wanted to emigrate to Canada. The poster was produced in 1927 by the Anchor-Donaldson shipping line, which was created in Glasgow in 1916.

Source A

ANCHOR-DONALDSON PASSENGERS ARE SATISFIED PASSENGERS
A-D

Urgently Wanted

600 MEN
FOR
CANADA

300 FOR WINNIPEG
FARE - £4 10/-
Single Men without experience
To sail between 15th July and 20th August

300 FOR TORONTO
FARE - £3 10/-
Single Men fully experienced
To arrive not later than 15th August

Situations Guaranteed at Good Wages

The only available sailing dates are:
"Letitia" 15th July
"Athenia" 29th July
"Andania" 6th Aug.

The necessary Application Forms can be obtained from
THIS AGENCY

How useful is Source A as evidence of the opportunities that attracted Scots to other lands?

(5 marks)

Here is a weak answer:

The source is useful because it shows an advert by the Anchor line shipping company. It tells us that Canada urgently needs 600 men. It also shows that jobs were available – 'situations guaranteed'. The source is useful because it shows that workers could earn 'good wages' in Canada. This shows the opportunities that were available due to the attractions of higher earnings in Canada, compared to Scotland.

Why is this a weak answer?

This answer is weak because:

(1) The answer fails to evaluate by referring to the origin and possible purpose of the source. It merely describes who produced the source.

(2) The answer mostly describes the content of the source.

(3) There is no attempt to identify gaps using recalled information.

Marks

- The candidate fails to evaluate or explore the usefulness of origin and purpose (0 marks).
- The first piece of content is described so it is difficult to credit this. The final sentence is doing just a little more by explaining the point about good wages being on offer to workers who went to Canada (1 mark).
- There is no recall (0 marks).

Total achieved: 1 mark out of 5.

Here is a much better answer:

Source A is very useful as evidence of the opportunities that attracted Scots to places like Canada. However, the source cannot explain all the opportunities that existed, so its usefulness will be limited by this.

The origin of the source is very useful as the Anchor-Donaldson line was set up in 1916 to encourage Scots to emigrate to Canada. It was in their interests to sell Canada as a destination as they gained the fares from the emigrants. This is very much the purpose of the source as it concentrates on the positive side of emigration and the obvious attractions of emigration. The content illustrates the opportunities that would attract the emigrants as it focuses on the high wages on offer and the employment opportunities available. To Scots struggling to find work in the 1920s this was very attractive. It also shows that Scots were 'urgently' needed which is useful as it further shows that there were jobs available.

Although the source shows us the way in which one shipping line was encouraging Scots to emigrate, it does not focus on the way in which governments abroad worked hard to get people to come to their countries. One important way in which governments attracted Scots abroad was by offering free grants of land. Many Scots were skilled farmers and were wanted as a result. Countries like Canada and Australia targeted Scottish farmers. Also, the source does not talk about how there were greater freedoms abroad. Many Scots were attracted by the opportunity of not having a landlord who would boss them about.

Overall the source is very useful at showing some of the opportunities that attracted Scots to leave their country. However, the source does not give a full picture of the many other opportunities that existed for Scots.

Why is this a much better answer?

It is a better answer because:

(1) It not only identifies the origin and purpose of the source, but it explains why each makes it a useful source (2 marks).

(2) It provides detail of why the content is useful. It does not just describe the source. The answer comments on the usefulness of the information (2 marks).

(3) It includes detailed recalled information that is tied to the question. The points are developed with relevant detail (2 marks).

(4) The answer finishes with a balanced evaluation of the source. While this is not necessary for full marks it leaves a positive impression in the marker's mind.

Marks

This answer scores highly simply by following the three stage marking scheme process. The maximum number of marks for a Type 1 question is 5 so even if this answer dropped a mark on a section, the writer would still gain full marks.

Now try it yourself

Source B is part of a letter from Godfrey MacKinnon, originally from Skye but now farming in Australia, to his friend John McDonald from Uist, dated 18 March 1864.

Source B

I had very hard work of it the first three years that I was in the country but now I can take it a little easier… I have done very well for all the time I have been in the Colony [Australia] compared to if I had been in Skye for the rest of my life, even if I lived for fifty years or more. I have got a beautiful piece of country and first rate stock of both, sheep, cattle and horses. I have gone to great expense with my sheep purchases. I even imported rams. It will pay me very well in a few years. I had a splendid amount of wool this season and I expect a better amount next year.

How useful is Source B in explaining the opportunities that attracted so many Scots to emigrate? (5 marks)

In your answer you should refer to:

- the origin and possible purpose of the source
- the content of the source
- recalled knowledge.

Question Type 2 – The Comparison Question

Here is an example of a source comparison question.

Source C is from Tom Gallacher, 'The Catholic Irish in Scotland: In Search of Identity' (1991).

Source C

In Glasgow the Irish dominated the unskilled labour market for generations, finding work after the 1840s as casual construction workers or dock labourers, coal heavers, and as sweated labour in textiles, and in the chemical and dyeing works which were badly polluting the city by mid-century. They were an indispensable mobile workforce whose contribution to the 'Second City of Empire' went largely unappreciated by contemporary chroniclers. It was the sporting field rather than the workplace which enabled the immigrant community to look outwards and begin interacting with the rest of Scottish society. The Irish in Scotland began to fully participate with the founding in 1887 of Celtic, a name that is as Scottish as it is Irish. The successes which Celtic quickly went on to acquire, culminating in six unbroken years as league champions from 1904 to 1910, produced an enormous feeling of pride within the Irish Catholic community.

Source D is from W. W. Knox's *Industrial Nation: Work, Culture and Society in Scotland, 1800 –Present* (1999).

Source D

Nearly half the female textile workers in Greenock in 1851 were Irish-born; and half the coal and ironstone miners of Coatbridge were of the same origin. Indeed, by mid-century over a third of the population of Coatbridge was Irish-born. Although most Irish workers were employed in unskilled, low paid occupations, there is evidence to suggest they were able to penetrate into skilled occupations, such as boilermakers. However, this was limited and many employers of skilled labour discriminated against the Catholic workers. Consumption of leisure also produced rivalries. The high levels of discrimination and prejudice against Irish Catholics saw them retreat into their own communities centred on the Catholic Church. The links between workplace, religion and recreation formed a culture from which total withdrawal was unlikely. These links were strengthened by the emergence of professional football. The original Celtic supporters' clubs, the Celtic brake clubs, required that members were also fully fledged members of the League of the Cross.

To what extent do Sources C and D agree about the contribution of Irish immigrants to Scotland? **(5 marks)**

You should compare the content overall and in detail.

Here is a weak answer:

Sources C and D are about the economic contribution of emigrants to the Scottish economy. They also talk about Celtic football club.

Source C tells about the contribution of the Irish to the Scottish economy and all the work the Irish did. It also talks about the way having Celtic football club let them relate to Scottish workers.

Source D also talks about how many Irish born workers were in Scotland. It is a bit different as it tells us about how Irish Celtic was and how important the Catholic Church was.

The sources are both about the role of the Irish worker in Scotland and how important Celtic football club is.

Why is this a weak answer?

This is a weak answer because:

(1) There is no attempt to introduce the answer with an overall comparison. The candidate simply describes the two sources.

(2) The writer describes each source in turn with no attempt to compare specific points between the sources.

Marks

No marks would be gained as there is no attempt to compare the two sources in a meaningful way.

Here is a much better answer:

Sources C and D agree to a large extent about the contribution of Irish immigrants to Scotland. The sources certainly agree on the economic contribution of the Irish in the West of Scotland as well as the fact that they were unappreciated at the time. However, there is also some disagreement over the cultural impact of the Irish, in particular the Irish Catholics and the role of Celtic football club.

Sources C and D clearly agree about the jobs that Irish immigrants did. These were largely unskilled as Source C says, 'the Irish would dominate the unskilled labour market, finding work as casual construction workers or dock labourers, coal heavers and in sweated textiles'. Source D agrees when it talks about the dominance of the Irish born women in textile factories in Greenock and the miners of Coatbridge. The sources also agree about the way in which the Irish were treated, although there is a slight difference of emphasis. Source C talks about how the work of the Irish was unappreciated at the time in Glasgow, whereas D speaks about how the Irish Catholics in particular were discriminated against in the workplace.

The real disagreements come with how the Irish community interacted with Scottish society through sport. Source C talks about how sport allowed the immigrant community to look outwards and began to interact with Scottish Society, whereas D speaks about the Catholic community withdrawing into itself and sport reinforcing their own culture. Therefore there is disagreement over this important issue. Sources C and D also disagree about the impact of Celtic football club as C emphasises the way in which Celtic was Scottish and Irish and gave great pride to the Irish Catholic community. D has a different view as it tells of how football reinforced the Irish Catholicism through the supporters clubs that existed.

Overall, Sources C and D agree about the economic impact of the immigrant Irish community, but disagree about the cultural impact they had in Scotland.

Why is this a good answer?

(1) The answer starts well with a developed overall comparison that shows understanding of the areas of agreement and disagreement between the two sources (2 marks).

(2) The answer then gives four distinct points of direct comparison (4 possible marks).

(3) The comparisons are relevant and connected to each other through relevant extraction of evidence from the two sources.

Marks

This answer gains 5 marks out of 5. The answer scores highly because the candidate has thought about the areas of agreement and disagreement then has sought to exemplify this. The overall conclusion is a nice touch, but would not gain any marks.

Now try it yourself

Source E is from Martin J. Mitchell, 'Irish Catholics in the West of Scotland' (2008).

Source E

Irish workers were heavily involved in the growth of trade unions of unskilled workers in the late nineteenth century. In 1889 the National Union of Dock Labourers was founded by two Irishmen, Richard McGhee and Edward McHugh. According to Kenefick, dockers in Glasgow were 'overwhelmingly Catholic Irish in composition'. Indeed, what is noticeable is that there was comparatively little open popular hostility to the immigrant presence. Not only did many Irish Catholics mix and associate with Scottish Protestants – a considerable number also married them. It is now apparent that by the end of the nineteenth century the issue of mixed marriages was one which greatly vexed the Catholic Church. It has been suggested that as the century progressed the Catholic Church developed institutions and organisations which locked Catholics into an isolated, self-contained 'cradle to grave' community.

Source F is from Foster, Houston and Madigan, *Sectarianism, Segregation and Politics on Clydeside in the Later Nineteenth Century* (2008).

Source F

Our conclusion was that job discrimination on Clydeside did not operate on a sectarian or religious basis. If there was any discrimination, it tended to operate against all Irish immigrants equally. Where there were exceptions, they appear to have been generated by the Irish themselves. Once on Clydeside there were attempts to introduce Belfast-style patterns of exclusion by monopolising certain unskilled workplaces. Lobban found that in Greenock Protestant immigrants tried to control access to labouring jobs in the cotton mills and refineries; Catholics tried to control labouring work in the docks. This did not work in Glasgow because unskilled workers – including Irish immigrants – were forming trade unions in the late 1880s. In terms of family size, the Protestant and Catholic Irish in Govan and Kinning Park were identical – but the great bulk of men from both religions were married to women born in Ireland.

To what extent do Sources E and F agree about the experience of Irish immigrants in Scotland?

(5 marks)

You should compare the content overall and in detail.

Question Type 3 – the 'How far...' Question

This is the question that asks about a specific part of an issue and wants to find out how much you know on the subject. A useful way to start and answer to this type of question is to say '**partly**'. That gives a basic answer to the question, 'How far...'

The source will provide relevant information but will not give the whole picture. That allows you to include other information relevant to the answer from your own knowledge in order to provide a full answer. These have to be substantial and explained points to be credited.

There are two phases to any answer to this type of question.

(1) You must select relevant points from the source and develop each point in terms of the question. This may mean you bring in recalled information to help explain the view, but this is not always necessary.

(2) You must then bring in your own knowledge to show there are other points relevant to the answer that are not in the sources. This part is worth up to 7 marks.

Here is an example of a 'how far' question:

Source G is from Jock Phillips and Terry Hearn, *Settlers: New Zealand Immigrants from England, Ireland and Scotland, 1800–1945* (1988).

Source G

Certainly in the early years of settlement, especially while the first generation remained dominant, there was evidence of Scots cultural traditions. The Presbyterian Church became entrenched as a dominant force in the south, and Highland shepherds for a time continued to speak Gaelic. The general pattern seems to be that once the first generation died, elements of Scots culture did not long survive if they remained exclusive to people of Scots heritage. However, because the Scots were consistently present in New Zealand in considerable numbers some of their traditions made the transition to general acceptance. There are two good examples: holidays and country shows. Scots celebration of New Year's Day did spread. Events held on that day, such as the Caledonian Games, began to attract wider audiences outside the Scots community. Events such as Highland dancing and playing the bagpipes survived into a broader community as a result. By the end of the nineteenth century in labour laws and common practice New Zealanders were recognising New Year's Day as a public holiday, while in England it remained a day of work.

How far does Source G illustrate the contribution of Scots to the religious and cultural development of the Empire?
(10 marks)

Use the source and recalled knowledge.

Here is a weak answer:

The source gives quite good evidence of the contribution of Scots to the religious and cultural development of the Empire. It says, 'Highland shepherds for a time continued to speak Gaelic', which shows the influence of the Scots in New Zealand.

The source says, 'Scots celebration of New Year's Day did spread. Events held on that day, such as the Caledonian Games, began to attract wider audiences outside the Scots community', which shows more influence of Scots in New Zealand.

It says at the beginning that the 'Presbyterian Church became a dominant force in the South.' This means that the Scottish church was important in the South.

It also says that New Year's Day became a public holiday in New Zealand while it remained a day of work in England.

Why is this a weak answer?

This answer is weak mainly because:

(1) The candidate has selected some information that is irrelevant to the question when it talks about the Highland shepherds speaking Gaelic for a time. This cannot be credited.

(2) The answer relies almost entirely on the information provided in the source.

(3) The answer describes the information without commenting on what it is illustrating.

(4) There is no recall looking at other parts of the Empire like Canada, Australia and India.

Marks

The candidate only uses the source and only selects two relevant points that are developed in the most basic of ways. This will only gain 2 marks.

There is no recall so 0 out of 7 is achieved.

Total achieved: 2 marks out of 10.

Here is a much better answer:

Source G only partly illustrates the contribution of Scots to the religious and cultural development of the Empire. However, the source does have some important points to make about the contribution of Scots to New Zealand's religious and cultural development. The source picks up the point about the Presbyterian Church becoming a dominant force in the south of New Zealand.

This is true as the Presbyterian Church provided help for immigrant Scots, and made an important contribution to cultural life in New Zealand by its support of education for all. This attention to education in other countries is not mentioned by the source. For example, the Canadian education system has a lot to thank the Scots for. Scots were very important in encouraging a broad university curriculum. Canadian universities like King's College encouraged practical subjects for study. It was the first Canadian university to offer a course in engineering, for example. This broader influence of the Scots is not mentioned in Source G.

The Scots' long term influence is then picked up by the source when it describes the influence of Scots in terms of the holidays taken in New Zealand. The fact that bagpipes and Scottish country dancing are popular is the example that is given, along with their celebration of New Year's Day. The Source explains that New Year's Day is a holiday in New Zealand and this comes from the large Scottish community influence there.

Although this influence is clearly of importance the source does not look at other parts of the Empire. India was an interesting example, and contrast, as Scots administrators decided to challenge centuries-old attitudes in India. For example it was a Scot, the Marquess of Dalhousie, who made great efforts to end the practice of suttee in India. This was when the wife would throw herself on the funeral pyre of her dead husband. Dalhousie took direct action to end this as well as the murder cult called the Thugee. These were important changes that Scots made to the culture of India.

Therefore, although Source G does tell about the important impact of Scots to the culture and religion of New Zealand it does not tell us their broader impact on the Empire. The source illustrates the changes to an extent.

Why is this a better answer?

This is a better answer because:

(1) Although not as long as it could be, the answer picks out important points from the source that are relevant to the example and explains their importance to the cultural and religious impact of Scots abroad.

(2) The answer explains the source view, but then skilfully extends the point about the impact of the Presbyterian Church using relevant recall about the Church in Canada.

(3) There is a link to relevant recall that contrasts the experience in New Zealand with that in India. This balances the views from the source.

Marks

- At least three relevant points from the source are extracted and explained (3 marks).
- The contextual development of the point about the Presbyterian Church in Canada with its broader education and exemplification (2 marks).
- Broader recall linked to the question (2 marks).

Total achieved: 7 marks out of 10.

Now try it yourself

Source H is by Martin J. Mitchell, 'Irish Catholics in the West of Scotland' (2008).

Source H

It is undeniable that Irish workers – Catholic and Protestant – were used to break strikes, and, as a result, incurred the anger of Scottish workers. However, most of the evidence of this relates to the coal and iron industries of Lanarkshire and Ayrshire. The vast majority of Irish workers in the nineteenth century were not employed in the mining industry and were not employed as strike-breakers. Furthermore, even in the mining districts of the west of Scotland, the Irish experience was more complex than some historians have suggested. There is evidence that some Irish workers participated in strikes to protect and improve their wages and conditions during the 1840s and 1850s. From the 1870s onwards Irish miners – Catholic and Protestant – were prominent both in the rank-and-file and in the leadership of miners' trade unions in Lanarkshire. For example, it has been estimated that by 1900 the Irish made up almost three-quarters of the total membership of the Lanarkshire Miners' Union.

How far does Source H explain the assimilation of immigrants into Scottish society?

(10 marks)

Use the source and recalled knowledge.

Question type 4 – The 'How fully...' Question

This is the question that asks about an overall issue and wants to find out how much you know on the subject. A useful way to start an answer to this type of question is to say '**partly**'. That gives a basic answer to the question, 'How fully...' As you can see the approach to this question is very similar to that for the 'How far...' question. The main difference is that it looks at the 'big' picture of the issue, rather than a smaller, specific sub-issue.

The source will provide relevant information but will not give the whole picture. That allows you to include other information relevant to the answer from your own knowledge in order to provide a full answer. These have to be substantial and explained points to be credited.

There are two phases to any answer to this type of question:

(1) You must select relevant points from the source and develop each point in terms of the question. This may mean you bring in recalled information to help explain the view, but this is not always necessary.

(2) You must then bring in your own knowledge to show there are other points relevant to the answer that are not in the source. This part is worth up to **7 marks**.

Here is an example of a 'How fully...' question:

Source I is from Allan Macinnes, Marjory Harper and Linda Fryer (eds), *Scotland and the Americas, c.1650–c.1939: A Documentary Source Book* (2002).

Source I

A significant minority of Scots not only achieved personal success in Canada, but played a key part in shaping the country's development, as explorers, financiers and politicians. Sir John A. Macdonald – the product of a relatively humble home in Glasgow – was five years old when he emigrated with his parents to Kingston, Ontario. He subsequently became a lawyer, and went into politics, initially as an opponent of the colonial government in 1847. Conscious of the ever-present threat from Canada's more powerful neighbour to the south, and totally opposed to separation from Britain, Macdonald's strategy as first Prime Minister of the new Dominion was to promote a transcontinental railway which would join the Atlantic to the Pacific, open up the west to settlers, and in the process strengthen and unite the fledgling country.

How fully does Source I describe the impact of Scots emigrants on the Empire?

(10 marks)

Use the source and recalled knowledge.

Here is a weak answer:

Source I tells about Scots in Canada. The source tells how Scots were successful in shaping the country's development.

John Macdonald was important. He was a Scot. He sensibly opposed Canada joining America and helped build a railway that went across Canada. This joined the Atlantic and Pacific oceans. It also helped unite and join up the new country of Canada.

Scots were also important in the development of Canada as they took jobs there. This was very attractive to Scots and many travelled there as a result. In fact if you were a Scots emigrant there were adverts that told about the railway and how you could help build it and how you could then get land to go with it. All of this was very attractive to Scots. This also attracted Scots to countries like Australia and New Zealand. In fact attracting Scots to these countries became big business and countries employed agents in Scotland.

Therefore Source I does tell us a lot about Scots in Canada, but tells us little about why many Scots were there in the first place.

Why is this a weak answer?

This is a weak answer because:

- The source is not evaluated in terms of the question asked. It is described.
- There is a general evaluation of John Macdonald being important and why he was important. This could be credited.
- The recall is all irrelevant to the question asked. The candidate has confused the question with one on Issue 1: why Scots emigrated. This cannot be credited even if it is accurate.

Marks

This answer would achieve 1 mark out of 10 at the most.

Here is a better answer:

Source I partly explains the impact of Scots emigrants on the Empire, but concentrates on Canada. The source is very full on the issue of Scots as explorers and financiers in Canada. Scots were involved in the important fur trade for example and were vital in providing finance for the development of the Canadian economy.

The source explains this well as it makes the important point that the Canadian government saw the building of the Trans-Continental railway as very important. Scots were behind this as the source explains, as John Macdonald was the political will behind the scheme. He saw the line as a way of uniting Canada and making sure that it was not taken over by America to the south. Scots were also very involved in the finance for the scheme with Scots-controlled or led banks in Montreal and London providing the money. The engineer for the route of the train across the plains and mountains of Canada was a Scot called Stamford Fleming. So the source provides good information on Canada, but does not look at the impact of Scots on other parts of the Empire and the sometimes negative impact they had.

Scots were involved in attacks on native people in the Empire. This was true in places like Australia in particular. Scots were good farmers and attractive to the governments of countries like Canada and Australia because they could develop the land and make money. As they did this in Australia they came into contact with the Aboriginal people who lived a nomadic existence. Scots farmers, along with others, attacked the Aborigines more than once and even massacred large numbers in places like Warrigal Creek.

Scots were also involved in grabbling land from the Maori people of New Zealand and this led to an eventual war with these people. The source does not mention these things.

Scots also had a very positive impact on the Empire, however. There is no doubt that many places in the Empire have an education system that is based on one introduced by the Scottish Presbyterian Church that arrived with the settlers. Universities and schools across the Empire from Canada to India have been set up by Scots and had a broad curriculum based on the Scottish model. Scots education meant that girls in parts of India began to receive an education, for example.

So, although the source tells us a lot about the Empire it is not a full account of the impact of the Scots abroad. The result is mixed, but Scots did do a lot of good overall.

Why is this a better answer?

(1) The source is used effectively in terms of the posed question.

(2) The parts of the source selected are explained and expanded on with relevant recall.

(3) The recall is directly related to the posed issue and gives a balanced view of the Scots abroad.

Marks

- The source is used effectively and relevant sections are extracted to answer the question. A couple of points are run together regarding the political and economic benefits of the railway which reduces its effectiveness (3 marks).

- The information in the source is contextualised effectively, particularly with the development of points about finance and engineering (2 marks).
- There is extensive recall about the impact of Scots on native societies (2 marks).
- There is extensive recall about the Scots role in developing education in places like Canada and India (2 marks).

Total achieved: 9 marks out of 10.

Now try it yourself

Source J is from an advert placed in the *John O'Groat Journal*, 22 January 1841, by Duncan McLennan, Emigrant Agent, Inverness.

Source J

Mr Brennan has the pleasure of announcing that arrangements have been made for a succession of ships in the course of the ensuing Spring, for the conveyance of Passengers from Cromarty, Thurso and any other place where a sufficient number of Passengers may offer, to ports in Nova Scotia and Lower Canada. We are able to give a full and accurate description of the country and its resources. Here it need only be remarked, the climate is excellent, the soil fertile, and the commodities of life abundant, they abound with numerous safe bays, and the coast in general affords fishing ground scarcely surpassed by any in the world. A Central Emigration Committee has been formed in Toronto, Upper Canada in order that, by constant communication and mutual arrangements, every facility may be offered to emigrants on their arrival, as to their location, settlement, and employment. Also, we forwarded last year, under the sanction of the government, upwards of 400 passengers from Cromarty and Thurso, all of whom arrived safe in upper Canada.

How fully does Source J show the reasons for the migration of Scots?
(10 marks)

Use the source and recalled knowledge.

References

Reference for sources

For all photographs please see page ii.

Chapter 1

Source 1.4 Michael Lynch *Scotland: A New History*, pp. 410–11

Source 1.5 adapted from T. M. Devine *The Scottish Nation, 1700–2000*, p. 252

Source 1.6 T.C. Smout *A Century of the Scottish People, 1830–1950*, p. 34

Source 1.7 T.C. Smout *A Century of the Scottish People, 1830–1950*, p. 34

Source 1.9 T.C. Smout *A Century of the Scottish People, 1830–1950*, p. 40

Chapter 2

Source 2.1 T.M. Devine *The Scottish Nation, 1700–2000*, p. 264

Source 2.3 quoted in T.C. Smout *A Century of the Scottish People, 1830–1950*, p. 11

Source 2.4 Michael Lynch *Scotland: A New History*, p. 371

Source 2.5 Eric Richards *The Highland Clearances*, p. 5

Source 2.7 Sir Archibald Gieke quoted in Eric Richards *The Highland Clearances*, p. 2

Source 2.8 Sir Archibald Gieke quoted in Eric Richards *The Highland Clearances*, p. 2

Source 2.9 quoted in T.C. Smout *A Century of the Scottish People, 1830–1950*, p. 60

Source 2.10 quoted in T.M. Devine *The Scottish Nation, 1700–2000*, p. 467

Source 2.11 Michael Lynch *Scotland: A New History*, pp. 379–80

Source 2.12 T.M. Devine *The Scottish Nation, 1700–2000*, p. 464

Source 2.13 T.M. Devine *The Scottish Nation, 1700–2000*, p. 466

Source 2.14 Marjorie Harper *Adventurers and Exiles: The Great Scottish Exodus*, p. 11

Source 2.15 Letter held in the National Library of Scotland

Source 2.18 Marjorie Harper *Adventurers and Exiles: The Great Scottish Exodus*, p. 71

Source 2.19 Marjorie Harper *Adventurers and Exiles: The Great Scottish Exodus*, p. 111

Source 2.20 Letter held in the National Library of Scotland

Source 2.21 Letter held in the National Library of Scotland

Source 2.23 *Inverness Journal*, 1 July 1842

Source 2.24 quoted in Marjorie Harper *Adventurers and Exiles: The Great Scottish Exodus*, p. 80

Source 2.26 quoted in Marjorie Harper *Adventurers and Exiles: The Great Scottish Exodus*, p. 50

Source 2.28 T.C. Smout *A Century of the Scottish People, 1830–1950*, pp. 61–2

Chapter 3

Source 3.2 Royal Commission on the Conditions of the Poorer Classes in Ireland, Appendix G, 'The State of the Irish Poor in Great Britain', Parliamentary Papers (1836), XXXIV, p. iii

Source 3.3 Royal Commission on the Conditions of the Poorer Classes in Ireland, Appendix G, 'The State of the Irish Poor in Great Britain', Parliamentary Papers (1836), XXXIV, p. iii

Source 3.4 T.C. Smout *A Century of the Scottish People, 1830–1950*, p. 91

Source 3.5 quoted in Mary Edward *Who belongs to Glasgow?* p. 45

Source 3.8 Graham Walker 'The Protestant Irish in Scotland', in T.M. Devine (ed.) *Irish Immigrants and Scottish Society in the Nineteenth and Twentieth Centuries*, p. 45

Source 3.9 Graham Walker 'The Protestant Irish in Scotland', in T.M. Devine (ed.) *Irish Immigrants and Scottish Society in the Nineteenth and Twentieth Centuries*, p. 51

Source 3.11 T.C. Smout *A Century of the Scottish People, 1830–1950*, pp. 99–100

Source 3.12 Graham Walker 'The Protestant Irish in Scotland', in T.M. Devine (ed.) *Irish Immigrants and Scottish Society in the Nineteenth and Twentieth Centuries*, p. 59

Source 3.13 T.C. Smout *A Century of the Scottish People, 1830–1950*, p. 154

Source 3.14 quoted in Billy Kay (ed.) *Odyssey: Voices from Scotland's recent past, Second Collection*, p. 114

Source 3.15 quoted in Billy Kay (ed.) *Odyssey: Voices from Scotland's recent past, Second Collection*, p. 114

Source 3.16 Kenneth Collins *Second City Jewry*, p. 40

Source 3.18 J.A. Hammerton *Sketches from Glasgow*, quoted in Billy Kay (ed.) *Odyssey: Voices from Scotland's recent past, Second Collection*, p. 115

Source 3.19 Murdoch Rodgers, in Billy Kay (ed.) *Odyssey: Voices from Scotland's recent past, Second Collection*, p. 114

Source 3.20 Kenneth Collins *Second City Jewry*, p. 10

Source 3.21 quoted in Billy Kay (ed.) *Odyssey: Voices from Scotland's recent past, Second Collection*, p. 118

Source 3.22 Murdoch Rodgers 'The Lithuanians', *History Today*, vol. 35, no. 7

Source 3.25 Murdoch Rodgers 'The Lithuanians', *History Today*, vol. 35, no. 7

Source 3.26 Joe Pieri *The Scots-Italians*, p. 14

Source 3.28 Joe Pieri *The Scots-Italians*, p. 63

Source 3.29 T.M. Devine *The Scottish Nation, 1700–2000*, pp. 515–16

Chapter 4

Source 4.1 T.M. Devine *The Scottish Nation, 1700–2000*, p. 471

Source 4.3 Jenni Calder *Scots in Canada*, p. 14

Source 4.5 David S. MacMillan 'The Scot as Businessman', in W. Stanford Reid (ed.) *The Scottish Tradition in Canada*, p. 180

Source 4.8 J.A. McIntyre 'The Scot as Farmer and Artisan', in W. Stanford Reid (ed.) *The Scottish Tradition in Canada*, p. 165

Source 4.9 J.A. McIntyre 'The Scot as Farmer and Artisan', in W. Stanford Reid (ed.) *The Scottish Tradition in Canada*, p. 170

Source 4.10 J.A. McIntyre 'The Scot as Farmer and Artisan', in W. Stanford Reid (ed.) *The Scottish Tradition in Canada*, p. 172

Source 4.13 Pierre Berton (1976) 'The National Dream', p. 319, quoted in W. Stanford Reid *The Scottish Tradition in Canada*, p. 202

Source 4.14 D.C. Masters 'The Scottish tradition in Higher Education', in W. Stanford Reid (ed.) *The Scottish Tradition in Canada*, p. 267

Source 4.15 Elizabeth Waterson 'The Lowland tradition in Canadian literature', in

W. Stanford Reid (ed.) *The Scottish Tradition in Canada*, p. 203

Source 4.16 George Emmerson 'The Gaelic tradition in Canadian culture', in W. Stanford Reid (ed.) *The Scottish Tradition in Canada*, p. 246

Source 4.18 Jenni Calder *Scots in Canada*, p. 84

Source 4.19 Arthur Herman *The Scottish Enlightenment: The Scots' Invention of the Modern World*, p. 357

Source 4.21 Malcolm Prentis *The Scots in Australia*, p. 95

Source 4.23 Malcolm Prentis *The Scots in Australia*, p. 107

Source 4.26 Malcolm Prentis *The Scots in Australia*, p. 174

Source 4.30 Jock Philips and Terry Hearn *Settlers: New Zealand Immigrants from England, Ireland and Scotland, 1800–1945*, p. 54

Source 4.31 Michael Fry *The Scottish Empire*, p. 226

Source 4.32 Jock Philips and Terry Hearn *Settlers: New Zealand Immigrants from England, Ireland and Scotland, 1800–1945*, p. 173

Source 4.35 Michael Fry *The Scottish Empire*, p. 232

Source 4.40 Alex Cain *The Cornchest for Scotland: Scots in India*, p. 17

Source 4.42 Michael Fry *The Scottish Empire*, p. 201

Source 4.43 Arthur Herman *The Scottish Enlightenment: The Scots' Invention of the Modern World*, p. 340

Source 4.45 Michael Fry *The Scottish Empire*, p. 197

Source 4.47 Bruce Lenman *An Economic History of Modern Scotland 1660–1976*, p. 207

Chapter 5

Source 5.1 T. M. Devine *Irish Immigrants and Scottish Society in the Nineteenth and Twentieth Centuries*, p. v

Source 5.4 John F. McCaffrey 'Irish Issues in the Nineteenth and Twentieth Century: Radicalism in a Scottish Context?', in T. M. Devine (ed.) (1991) *Irish Immigrants and Scottish Society in the Nineteenth and Twentieth Centuries*, p. 126

Source 5.7 Joe Pieri *The Scots-Italians*, p. 15

Source 5.10 Joe Pieri *The Scots-Italians*, p. 15

Source 5.12 Kenneth Collins *Second City Jewry*, p. 111

Source 5.14 T.M. Devine *The Scottish Nation, 1700–2000*, p. 254

Source 5.18 Bruce Lenman *An Economic History of Modern Scotland 1660–1976*, p. 193

Source 5.19 Marjory Harper *Adventurers and Exiles: The Great Scottish Exodus*, p. 306

Source 5.20 Marjory Harper *Adventurers and Exiles: The Great Scottish Exodus*, p. 287

Source 5.21 Ewan A. Cameron *Impaled upon a Thistle: Scotland since 1880*, p. 103

Source 5.22 Hew Strachan 'Scotland's Military Identity', *Scottish Historical Review*, Vol. 85, Number 2: No. 220, pp. 326–7

Source 5.25 Bruce Lenman *An Economic History of Modern Scotland 1660–1976*, p. 223

Chapter 6

Source 6.3 Michael Lynch *Scotland: A New History*, p. 374

Source 6.4 Jock Philips and Terry Hearn *Settlers: New Zealand Immigrants from England, Ireland and Scotland, 1800–1945*, pp. 168–9

Source 6.7 Michael Lynch *Scotland: A New History*, p. 374

Source 6.8 Hew Strachan 'Scotland's Military Identity', *Scottish Historical Review*, Vol. 85, Number 2: No. 220, p. 328

Source 6.9 Tom Devine *Scotland's Empire*, p. xxvii

Preparing for Paper 2

Source B quoted in Marjorie Harper *Adventurers and Exiles: The Great Scottish Exodus*, p. 256

Source C quoted in T.M. Devine (ed.) *Irish Immigrants and Scottish Society in the Nineteenth and Twentieth Centuries*, pp. 21–26

Source D W.W. Knox *Industrial Nation: Work, Culture and Society in Scotland, 1800–Present*, pp.142–143

Source E Martin J. Mitchell 'Irish Catholics in the West of Scotland', in M.J. Mitchell (ed.) New Perspectives on the Irish in Scotland, pp. 4–10

Source F J. Foster, M. Houston and C. Madigan 'Sectarianism, Segregation and Politics on Clydeside in the Later Nineteenth Century', in M.J. Mitchell (ed.) *New Perspectives on The Irish in Scotland*, pp. 68

Source G Jock Phillips and Terry Hearn *Settlers: New Zealand Immigrants from England, Ireland and Scotland, 1800–1945*, pp.169–171

Source H quoted in Martin J. Mitchell (ed.) *New Perspectives on the Irish in Scotland*, p.7

Source I Marjory Harper, Linda Fryer and Allan Macinnes (eds) *Scotland and the Americas, c. 1650-c.1939: A Documentary Source Book*, pp. 84–85

Source J Duncan McLennan Advert in *John O'Groat Journal*

Bibliography

Cain, A. (1986) *The Cornchest for Scotland: Scots in India*, National Library of Scotland

Calder, J. (2003) *Scots in Canada*, Luath

Cameron, E.A. (2010) *Impaled upon a Thistle: Scotland since 1880*, Edinburgh University Press

Collins, K. (1990) *Second City Jewry*, Scottish Jewish Archives Committee

Devine, T.M., ed. (1991) *Irish Immigrants and Scottish Society in the Nineteenth and Twentieth Centuries*, John Donald

Devine, T.M., ed. (1992) *Scottish Emigration and Scottish Society,* John Donald

Devine, T.M. (1999) *The Scottish Nation, 1700–2000*, Penguin

Devine, T.M. (2003) *Scotland's Empire,* Allen Lane

Edward, M. (2007) *Who Belongs to Glasgow?* (Revised edition) Luath Press Ltd

Emmerson, G. (1976) 'The Gaelic Tradition in Canadian Culture', in W. Stanford Reid (ed.) *The Scottish Tradition in Canada*, McClelland and Stewart

Fry, M. (2001) *The Scottish Empire*, Tuckwell Press

Harper, M. (2003) *Adventurers and Exiles: The Great Scottish Exodus*, Profile Books

Harper, M., Fryer, L. and Macinnes, A., eds (2002) *Scotland and the Americas, c. 1650–c.1939: A Documentary Source Book*, Scottish History Society

Herman, A. (2001) *The Scottish Enlightenment: The Scots' Invention of the Modern World*, Fourth Estate

Kay, B., ed. (1982) *Odyssey: Voices from Scotland's Recent Past, Second Collection*, Polygon

Knox, W.W. (1999) *Industrial Nation: Work, Culture and Society in Scotland, 1800–Present*, Edinburgh University Press

Lenman, B. (1977) *An Economic History of Modern Scotland 1660–1976*, B.T. Batsford

Lynch, M. (1991) *Scotland: A New History*, Pimlico

Masters, D.C. (1976) 'The Scottish Tradition in Higher Education', in W. Stanford Reid (ed.) *The Scottish Tradition in Canada*, McClelland and Stewart

McCaffrey, J.F. (1991) 'Irish Issues in the Nineteenth and Twentieth Century: Radicalism in a Scottish Context?', in T. M. Devine (ed.) (1991) *Irish Immigrants and Scottish Society in the Nineteenth and Twentieth Centuries*, John Donald

McIntyre, J.A. (1976) 'The Scot as Farmer and Artisan' in W. Stanford Reid (ed.) *The Scottish Tradition in Canada*, McClelland and Stewart

McLennan, D. (1841) Advert in *John O'Groat Journal*

MacMillan, D.S. (1976) 'The Scot as Businessman', in W. Stanford Reid (ed.) *The Scottish Tradition in Canada*, McClelland and Stewart

Mitchell, M.J. (1998) *The Irish in the West of Scotland, 1797–1848: Trade Unions, Strikes and Political Movements,* John Donald

Mitchell, M.J., ed. (2008) *New Perspectives on the Irish in Scotland,* John Donald

Philips, J. and Hearn, T. (1988) *Settlers: New Zealand Immigrants from England, Ireland and Scotland, 1800–1945*, Auckland University Press

Pieri, J. (2005) *The Scots-Italians*, Mercat Press

Prentis, M. (2008) *The Scots in Australia*, University of New South Wales Press

Reid, W.S., ed. (1976) *The Scottish Tradition in Canada*, McClelland and Stewart

Richards, E. (2007) *The Highland Clearances,* Birlinn

Rodgers, M. (1985) 'The Lithuanians', *History Today*, vol. 35, issue 7

Royal Commission on the Conditions of the Poorer Classes in Ireland (1836) Appendix G, 'The State of the Irish Poor in Great Britain', Parliamentary Papers, XXXIV

Smout, T.C. (1986) *A Century of the Scottish People, 1830–1950*, Fontana

Strachan, H. (2006) 'Scotland's Military Identity', *Scottish Historical Review*, Vol. 85, No. 2

Walker, G. (1991) 'The Protestant Irish in Scotland', in T.M. Devine (ed.) *Irish Immigrants and Scottish Society in the Nineteenth and Twentieth Centuries*, John Donald

Waterson, E. (1976) 'The Lowland Tradition in Canadian Literature', in W. Stanford Reid (ed.) *The Scottish Tradition in Canada*, McClelland and Stewart

Index